Team Strategies for Success

Doing What Counts in Education

Mary Ann Smialek

scarecrow
education

The Scarecrow Press, Inc.
A Scarecrow Education Book
Lanham, Maryland, and London
2001

SCARECROW PRESS, INC.
A SCARECROW EDUCATION BOOK

Published in the United States of America
by Scarecrow Press, Inc.
4720 Boston Way, Lanham, Maryland 20706
www.scarecroweducation.com

4 Pleydell Gardens, Folkestone
Kent CT20 2DN, England

British Library Cataloguing in Publication Information Available

Library of Congress Cataloging-in-Publication Data

Smialek, Mary Ann, 1946–
    Team strategies for success : doing what counts in education /
    Mary Ann Smialek.
        p.   cm.—(A Scarecrow education book)
    Includes bibliographical references (p.) and index.
    ISBN 0-8108-4064-2 (alk. paper)—ISBN 0-8108-4065-0 (pbk. : alk. paper)
    1. School management teams—United States.   2. School management and
organization—United States.   3. Educational leadership—United States.
4. Educational change—United States.   I. Title.   II. Series.
LB2806.3 .S65   2001
371.2′00973—dc21   2001031079

Contents

Acknowledgments   iv

Introduction: Background of the Team Challenge in Education   v

Part One: Considering the Team Approach   1

1   Accepting the Challenge   3

Part Two: Setting the Stage for Teams   11

2   Team Environment Considerations   13

3   Dimensions of Teams   21

Part Three: What's Happening in Teams?   31

4   Current Team Efforts   33

Part Four: Building Successful Teams   47

5   Simple and Easy Strategies That Work   49

6   Team Empowerment: How Do You Get It Right?   61

Glossary   95

Reference List   97

Index   107

About the Author   111

Acknowledgments

I would like to express my sincere gratitude to those special people who have supported and encouraged me in their own unique way throughout this endeavor: To my mom, Ann Platek, for her prayers and neverending encouragement; to my husband, Bob, for his sound advice, belief in me, and acceptance of my commitment to my goals; to my son for his computer expertise—remember, Rob, that I'm proud of you, too; to Wendy Truman for her sustained efforts as well as expert typing and formatting skills for the many edits of this venture; and to my sister, Joanne Utchell, who supported my efforts from their inception through the early stages of my research. She is the one person I relied on for suggestions, personal and professional, and above all the laughter that put everything in perspective.

Introduction

Background of the Team Challenge in Education

More now than ever, U.S. schools are on the verge of substantive change. New challenges and opportunities arise every day to move schools closer to a transformational change rather than just a transitional one. Until now, schools have attempted to adopt change into the existing systems and structures of education. This book offers strategies to facilitate transformative change in education through empowered teams. This transformation focuses on a new leadership philosophy that encompasses three crucial elements: a vision for education that bridges the gap between what is and what will be, a leadership commitment, and active participation of staff.

To meet the challenges and discover the opportunities to bring about needed educational change, school leaders must act in unaccustomed and unconventional ways. After creating and sharing a vision for the future, educational leaders face the ultimate challenge: They must attract others to common purposes and empower them to act. Once the vision is articulated and communicated, actively involving others in planning, problem solving, and implementing solutions is the next crucial step forward in initiating change in education. Fostering collaborative efforts and strengthening others toward active involvement are necessary to revitalize schools.

The content of this book has a rational theme in both theory and practice. This fact constitutes the strength of this exposé on teams in education. Teams, which have been adopted by a diverse cross section of business and industry, have not yet been accepted in educational circles. The fact remains, however, that teaming is not yet a common practice—even though school reform literature is teeming with shouts of building relationships between schools and their clients, of developing teams, and of redefining the role of school leaders to help educational organizations move toward their goals by continuously improving working processes.

Shrinking budgets, fewer resources, growing demands on staff, insufficient family support, and vague, ever-changing guidelines and regulations reinforce the need to achieve quality in schools and to bring about a significant change for the better in education today. Educational program quality, however, will not happen with only the administration involved. Teachers, parents, support staff, and students must participate together. As schools become more involved in their journey toward quality, they discover the benefits of having people at all levels of the organization working together in problem-solving and shared decision-making ventures.

The more teams believe that they can influence and guide the organization, the greater the organizational effectiveness, and satisfaction will be the result. Shared power results in heightened job satisfaction and performance throughout the school system. When a process makes people feel that they have a voice in matters that affect them, they will have a greater commitment to the overall enterprise and will take greater responsibility for what happens in the organization. Effective educational leaders cannot do everything by themselves. They must allow staff members to assist in the process of attaining organizational goals. As educational leaders empower others, a ripple effect results by actually increasing leadership power. Power at various educational levels could and should be shared, delegated, and transferred with flexible guidelines. The more power that is shared with staff, the more power a leader possesses, thus producing an empowerment cycle that comes full circle. As leaders delegate their power and responsibility to others, a cooperative and cyclical process results. Since leaders have more time to spend in other areas, their competencies are increased so their own influence can be furthered, and, thus, more power and responsibility can be given to others.

The problems in American education lie primarily in the way the school system is structured and run. Treating staff members as professionals; including parents, students, community members, and school board members on teams; listening to their suggestions; and encouraging them to engage in constant self-improvement through team-building processes are the basis of a leadership that will effect significant educational change. If true change is to be achieved, it will require not only careful planning but a new type of educational leader who is patient and committed to shared decision making in and through the implementation of teams.

Will America's school leaders accept the challenge of shared leadership through the use of teams? It will take time to evolve and be recognized and accepted as not only a strategic process but one that can bring about an educational system that is intrinsically and extrinsically the best that it can be, an educational system that will become the pivotal point in keeping our society intellectually and economically competitive by enhancing both individual and organizational success.

The purpose and challenge of this book is to provide educators with a primer, a first book of quality team considerations and strategies for success. The transformation to an environment in which teams make decisions and find solutions to problems that directly affect them and their clients will move schools forward into substantive changes. These changes will affect the public and political perceptions of whether U.S. schools are capable of providing the knowledge and skills students need to enter the increasingly sophisticated workplace of the Information Age. While this book was written specifically for education leaders, administrators, principals, teachers, and guidance counselors, it can also be of assistance to business and industry leaders, parents, school board members, and those who are interested in facilitating quality improvement in our schools.

Hopefully, it will serve as the change agent to bring about an awareness of the benefits of people at all levels of the school organization and their clients working together in team-building environments. Seven steps for successfully developing and implementing empowered teams in education are presented. Highlighted is the team empowerment model, an action plan based on the premise that educational teams are composed of a number of interrelated processes that cannot be influenced independently of each other. It is offered as a workable design to empower teams in education. Its structure promotes the desired outcomes to break down the barriers within school organizations so that leaders, staff, and clients will be part of one team dedicated to the continuous pursuit of educational quality.

Part One

CONSIDERING THE TEAM APPROACH

CHAPTER 1

Accepting the Challenge

When you do the same thing over and over again, in exactly the same way, don't expect the results to be different.

Will you as an educational leader accept the challenge to lead in unaccustomed and unconventional ways with teams? You want to accept this challenge, but you are stopped when your thoughts echo the question: Will teams really make a difference in my school district? Your school district can change for the better with teams, but up until now you just haven't had the tools and the focus to make this a reality.

Consider taking the following steps and applying the team strategies outlined in this book for more successful students, schools, and work environments, and for rewarding client partnerships in education. If what you're doing now isn't working, it would be in your best interest to try an alternative approach to change. You can start by admitting you do not know everything you must in order to get the results that you want in your district.

To start, you need to have an open mind. Ask yourself right now: Do we really have a strategy to ensure continuous improvement in the school district? Is the district really headed in the right direction? Are we doing today what we did yesterday only because we did it that way last month, last year?

The ultimate challenge for educational leaders today is redesigning the systems and structures that will ensure continuous improvement in their districts. Teams facilitate this endeavor. It is not as overwhelming as it sounds because the responsibility for securing that this happens rests not with just one person but with everyone who has an interest in the future of education in your school district.

Of course, your district needs a leader with a vision who shares leadership with teams—a proven practice in both business and industry that can be applied to an educational environment seeking to improve work processes.

Someone in your district has to champion the cause for teams. Is that person you? It may not always be easy, but the rewards will outweigh the drawbacks if you just get started.

Your district's success in this challenge can effectively begin with the consideration and acceptance of a team approach to change. District teams, designed to deliver the competencies necessary for students to become responsible members of the twenty-first century, are the vehicle with which to facilitate the needed change.

Our job, as educational leaders, is to break down the tasks of initiation and implementation into workable and measurable units. Striving to have all clients of education on the same page and aligning our education system around the components of continuous improvement through teaming processes are important. We can gather the evidence that supports the belief that all children—along with their parents, teachers, and other community members—can learn that through shared problem-solving and decision-making techniques. A quality team approach has much to offer education.

However, keep in mind that the work of continuous improvement in teams is just that—continuous. It has no end point. It is the work of a lifetime. Systemic change takes time. Now is the time to begin on your journey.

Your ability to improve education in your district is based on support partnerships, which require that the community be knowledgeable about the business of your schools, mainly the achievement of your students and all that it entails. Systemic reform requires a rethinking of the role of the community in the work of schools. Board members, parents, and community members must be informed about the real challenges of schools in order for you to maintain the support necessary to attain and sustain quality education.

School leaders are only beginning to understand the power of teams in education and to put them into practice. They are starting to use teams to prepare staff and students to better cope with a new world of work and its ever-changing marketplace. Many leaders in education are skeptical, some are closed-minded, some have an attitude of resistance.

Those who are at least willing to give teams in education a chance have a chance to initiate change for the better and to facilitate continuous improvement in their districts. Are you ready for the challenge?

Having read what you've read so far, you've arrived at a crossroads. You will soon be making a decision that will chart your district's future. Will you accept the challenge of teams in your district?

First, it is crucial to understand a basic concept of teamwork: Everyone has a vital role in the educational system. This concept allows that team members figure out what their goals should be and what kinds of problems they should be looking for, where to look for them, and what solutions are important. Consider the fact that the people at the level where the work gets done best know where the problems lie.

Professional and support staff, parents, and students working in teams are the essential instruments in understanding what is happening at the places where the work gets done. They must know how to determine which problems are caused by the overall system itself. Therefore, everyone in the system is involved in studying it and proposing ideas on how to improve it. Learning is part of work, driven by each person's need to be effective. The building and district problem-solving and shared decision-making processes address the same problem: how to meet the learning needs of children. Due to the systemic connections between the two, problem solving becomes a process for which everyone is responsible but no one individual is to blame.

As leaders in education begin to adopt the use of teams, they are discovering the good news and the bad news. Teams in education are neither a "quick fix" nor a "magic act." Teams cannot be successful if they are viewed as the "flavor of the month" or as "our project for this school year."

The real rewards begin to emerge when team processes become so embedded in the culture of the school organization, the day-to-day work of its people and systems, that they simply become "the way we do things around here." The greatest benefits come about naturally as a part of the evolutionary process of implementing a program of continuous improvement in a consistent manner, through the use of teams.

The benefits of teams are tangible: People feel better about themselves and their efforts on the job, and they take greater pride in their work. Relationships among people in the organization are honest and open. Educational leaders often feel less isolated and misunderstood. Productivity goes up as work processes are improved continuously.

Teams have another distinct advantage over solo efforts: the mutual support and synergy that arise between team members. Continuous improvement is hard work and takes a long time. It is all too easy for one person's commitment and enthusiasm to falter during a long project. It will be difficult for any one educational staff member to find the time and energy to consistently devote to a continuous improvement effort. However, when people work together productively on an important project, they usually have enough energy to sustain their enthusiasm and support it through difficult times and hectic school schedules.

As a spirit of teamwork takes root, staff at various levels of the school district will begin working together toward educational quality through continuous improvement—all one team moving together in the same direction. This need not be a fantasy.

Business, industry, and service organizations already have shown that improvement results require consistent leadership, effective systemic management, and a common belief-based framework for understanding among all members of the team. As connections, relationships, and possibilities already inherent in the organization appear through the team structure as fundamental rather than incremental, changes will begin to happen. Because change reinforces natural inclinations and beliefs, the implementation of more effective and satisfying ways of getting things done won't have to wait for all the elements to be in place before starting.

Educational program quality will only happen if the staff—at all organizational levels—is involved. Working together in teams encourages staff empowerment, creates a sense of ownership, and produces responsiveness to the pursuit of continuous improvement in educational services. Team building shapes the staff's leadership and fosters collaboration by providing various school groups with the power necessary to make a difference. Teamwork improves both instruction and curriculum and enables continuous improvement in the delivery of student services. As school systems facilitate collaborative work environments in which staff have a say in conditions affecting their work lives, team members are responsible for contributing as fully as possible by sharing their knowledge and expertise. This holistic approach is characteristic of the entire search for educational quality.

The success or failure of a team's school improvement endeavors will have great impact on the entire school district because teams are highly visible entities. It is necessary to clearly understand where teams fit into the overall restructuring and improvement plans of the school district and how to use them properly. Scholtes (1994) emphasizes that a team's real importance is the reeducation of all school system personnel and that this process cannot be underestimated.

This book focuses on cross-functional project teams in education. I have often been asked how administrative cross-functional project teams differ from classroom cooperative-learning teams. In the following, I make their differences clear.

Cross-functional teams are made up of groups of individuals functioning at various levels in the educational process in a school district that come together to focus on the continuous improvement of the system. A successful project team requires the input and cooperation of its members. Before this type of team can function efficiently, knowledge of basic concepts (e.g., processes and systems, internal and external clients) and the use of the tools of the scientific approach (e.g., flow charts, Pareto charts, cause-and-effect diagrams) are necessary. Team members examine the learning process using these quality-improvement techniques. Processes, instead of unrelated events, are studied. Team members look for problems in processes and for possible solutions that they have the ability to implement. Strategies are offered to project team members in order to improve teaming practices within this broader team approach to improving educational processes and solving administrative and instructional problems.

Classroom cooperative-learning teams, on the other hand, are made up of students in a classroom working together rather than alone. Collaborative-learning-team classrooms operate based on three important principles:

- Cooperative skills are taught and practiced, and feedback is given on how well the skills were used in the group.
- Class members are encouraged to operate as a cohesive group.

- Class members are given responsibility for their own learning and behavior.

Class members are also involved in negotiation and decision making about curriculum content in their classroom, classroom rules and consequences, and timetables.

Cooperative skills that class members learn and practice include the following:

- Forming groups
- Working as a group
- Problem solving
- Managing differences

The process of teaching the skills is the same for all: Make the skills explicit, provide practice, give feedback, and encourage reflection. These skills foster both intellectual and social development over more traditional individualized and competitive learning environments.

Classroom cooperative-learning teams are microcosms of the much broader organizational cross-functional teams. The skills learned in the cooperative classroom are important prerequisites to the skills needed in the more sophisticated cross-functional project teams of the professional workplace.

Is your current method of leadership working in your school district? Are you willing to move your position? There never is a "best time," so there's no better time than right now to adopt the team approach to continuous improvement in your district. There's no better place than right here. It's not too late. Whatever your situation, you deserve to give teams a chance. You will be surprised at the positive results—even some you can't even imagine now—that you will attain.

As you begin on your team journey, remember two truths. First, you've got what it takes to initiate teams in your district. Second, nobody is going to do it for you.

Team Strategies for Success is at the core of what you need to know. In this book you are presented with the essential knowledge for implementing and maintaining successful teams in your district. Now, it's up to you.

PLAN-DO-STUDY-ACT CYCLE

The Plan-Do-Study-Act (PDSA) cycle (see figure 1.1) forms the basis for team efforts in problem solving. It represents the four steps necessary to address a desired system or process change:

1. Plan a change or a test aimed at improvement.
2. Carry it out, preferably on a small scale.
3. Study the results. What did we learn?
4. Act on the results. Adopt the change, abandon it, or run through the cycle again, possibly under different environmental conditions.

Even at these early stages of considering team initiation, it would be helpful to use the PDSA cycle, or *Shewhart Cycle*. The concept came to industry from education, from John Dewey himself. Shewhart derived the PDSA cycle from Dewey's emphasis on meeting regularly to discuss progress and innovation always with the intention of refining efforts relative to results.

Step 1: The first step is developing a *plan* or process to study and

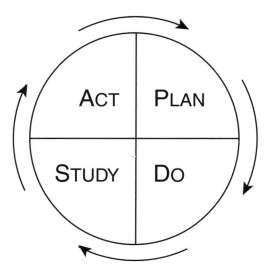

Figure 1.1   *The PDSA cycle.*

analyze (e.g., the way you will choose team members). What can be done to improve it? First, you must organize the team to develop the plan. Then you can determine what data you currently have, what additional data you will need to assess the improvement, and possibly how the data will be used. You cannot proceed without a plan.

Step 2: *Do* it. Carry out the plan, make the improvement, preferably on a small scale or pilot basis.

Step 3: *Study* or check the data on the effects of the improvement or innovation.

Step 4: *Act* on what the pilot program teaches you. Either carry out the innovation on a permanent basis, discard the innovation, or go back to step 1 by modifying or refining the innovation and gathering new data on its effectiveness as you make modifications and adjustments to it.

Part Two

SETTING THE STAGE FOR TEAMS

CHAPTER 2

Team Environment Considerations

STAFF EMPOWERMENT

Staff empowerment is a new conception of leadership and power relationships.

When implementing teams as a school leader, first you must influence the action toward staff empowerment. Recognize, create, and channel your own power by giving your staff the authority to make decisions. Think big. Start small. Implement one team. Be patient. Be persistent. Involve key people. Educate them. Make them believers. Success will follow. A collaborative environment in which team members are supported by trust, respect, and recognition can facilitate the empowerment process.

Improvements in the quality of education through teams must come from enhancing and strengthening the professional roles of your staff. Maximize their abilities and opportunities to exercise judgment and permit them to make decisions about reshaping and upgrading their working environment. Remember, none of these improvements can be made without strengthening your own education leadership. A new educational leadership that focuses on continuous improvement and that employs new ways of thinking and acting needs to be established in our school districts. This is in your power. At a time when business and industry have moved to greater worker participation in management, it seems only fair that educators too have their say in conditions that affect their work lives.

New ways of governing schools require new ways of conceptualizing school leadership. The use of teams in schools promotes fundamental changes in the ways that staff members are involved in leadership and decision-making issues. Subscribing to the definition of *empowerment* as a new conception of leadership hierarchy and power relationships is very motivating in getting the team concept started. When principles of collaboration are taken seriously, leadership can come from many sources: administrators, teachers, parents, and district support staff working in teams. As an educational leader, you must have confidence in your own abilities first to permit the concept of team empowerment to take root in your school district.

In the past, school leadership evolved from the principles defined by successful managers in successful corporations. Organizational roles were clearly defined by position. Board members, superintendents, principals, and teachers knew what their charges were for educating students prior to this era of calls for educational improvement. The principles of scientific management utilized to improve industrial production were no less reliable in improving educational production prior to the year 2001. Times have changed, and so must the schools and the people who do the business of guiding and teaching in them. It may take weeks or months before you see measurable results once you make the commitment to teams, but just remember that you will see results. Your team projects will lead to substantial improvements over time if you persist. Are you willing to empower your staff and support shared decision making? If so, read on.

TEAM LEADERSHIP

> Team leadership comes from many sources: administrators, staff, parents, community members, and even students.

A quality educational leader knows all involved must have a consistent view of the system that allows them to understand their fit and relationship to its outcomes. This leader knows everyone must speak a common language and have a common model for understanding how children learn and how the work of the system relates to it.

In an environment guided by the new team leadership, teams have the necessary time, training, and information to better understand the clients whose needs they respond to and the range of responses appropriate to each client's needs. If there is to be a community of leaders in a school, as an administrator, you must provide the staff with opportunities to take on more responsibilities, to have decision-making power in teams, and to be accountable for the results. Another consideration for you as an educational leader is to recognize the pitfalls of putting individuals into positions of responsibility with little sensitivity to prevailing conditions and little understanding of what it takes to create a staff development experience with genuine collegiality.

Real team leadership arises when you are more concerned about getting overall cooperation and energetic participation from organization members rather than getting particular tasks performed. If you are working in a cultural setting in which goals are unclear or organizational members do not agree about them, effective leadership requires an approach that transforms the feelings, attitudes, and beliefs of staff. Compliance is not enough under these circumstances; it is important to get team members to believe in themselves and in the goals of the organization. Team leaders are people-oriented. Rather than focus on task completion and performance, they build relationships and help teams develop goals and identify strategies for their accomplishment.

Team leadership is needed when you, as leader, discover the system is no longer effective and must figure out how to change it. Survival in business and industry and also the viability of America's public school system require that we have people throughout the organization who can both manage and lead. If we equate leadership with formal position, we disregard the complex, cooperative relationships among a number of people that are required to get things done or change the way they are done. The real intellectual challenge of understanding the nature of this new leadership is to try to capture, measure, observe, discuss, and treat engagement among staff who are trying to solve problems with support and openness. If you don't intend to do this, teaming is not the strategy for change in your district. Team leadership is contextual, and it is important for you, as an educational leader, to have a deep understanding of the culture of your organization. Effective educational leadership requires a supportive culture. To that end, as a leader, you must be able to identify cultural themes, values, and dreams with which staff can identify and internalize. The principles of this type of leadership include a client focus through teamwork enabled by the support of continued education and staff development training.

Developing team leadership requires a shift in emphasis. Adults only grow as leaders if they are reasonably self-aware and have organizational programs designed with components in which all team members look at themselves to see who they really are, what they really value, and how to interact with others. School leaders, as well as staff, must be confident in their own abilities to be effective leaders for this new team leadership. Team training backed by support and openness will achieve this goal of confidence.

One issue that is shared across American society is an urgent need to create organizations that are equal to today's complex challenges. We need to redefine leadership in human, moral, and spiritual terms. We need to reconsider and redesign leadership development and current educational systems and structures. We need to rethink and restructure school systems to encourage the kind of leadership that can help transform schools from past practices and patterns to those that will be needed to shape a successful future for education. Teams can help make this a reality.

Part of being successful in guiding team processes is first hanging in there and sticking with it. Many educational practitioners get impatient, quit too early, and fall short of success. There is a delicate balance between perseverance and a willingness to make necessary changes. You need the wisdom to know when to quit and when to stay right where you are. If you're quitting too early, remind yourself to persevere. Any new venture that is destined for success is going to take work and a sustained effort. If it didn't, your success wouldn't be as rewarding.

Plus/Delta Strategy

A plus/delta strategy (see figure 2.1) is a great way to close the day, a team meeting, or a project. Discuss what went well and what didn't. Record every response. Don't comment on responses, but do work on the deltas.

TEAM TRAINING

Team success is never an accident. It is always the result of intelligent effort, planning, and necessary training.

As school districts move toward teaming processes, there is recognition that most school personnel have had little training or experience work-

+	$\triangle$
Everyone was on time	Data collection
Meeting ended on time	Too many interruptions

Figure 2.1 *Sample of a plus/delta document.*

ing within schools on organized decision-making teams. Collaborative teaming requires skills, abilities, and certain conditions. The manner in which you need to lead involves the complex process of building these conditions whereby behavior is influenced less by direct leadership and more by a commitment to shared values.

The role of the district leader is changing from that of a manager of people to that of a facilitator and coach. Staff development programs must recognize the need to develop the process skills that team leaders and team members must utilize in working with people for making better decisions about teaching and learning within the school organization. *Coach, team builder,* and *facilitator* are terms descriptive of the emerging role educational leaders have in developing a collaborative culture within schools.

Our thinking about organizations and the nature of leadership is changing slowly in education. Attention is shifting from the enticement of external rewards to intrinsic motivators springing from the work itself. As we let go of machine models of work, we must see ourselves in new ways. To tap these intrinsic motivators, school leaders, as well as staff, need both technical expertise and extensive facilitative interpersonal skills.

It is imperative that educational systems create structures for working together in order to create conditions for continuous improvement. Collaboration has not been supported by school systems as a permanent structural condition. School systems have made collaboration an informal process for making decisions and working together. The governing process and formal structure of the educational organization are weighed toward centralized authority and limited decision making. Collaboration has been made an expectation for people but not for the school system. Now it is important that personnel experience this collaborative process in a real way in well-planned training programs.

Is team training really all that important? The answer is a resounding *yes*. My research (Smialek, 1996) has proven this to be the number one consideration for ensuring the success of teams in education. With the necessary technical and interpersonal skills training, teams establish communication and understanding of quality solutions across functional lines. Teams promote multiple points of view on any problem. They stimulate broader understandings of concerns and responsibility for quality. Teams develop cooperative attitudes between people and groups. Teams make the implementation of solutions easier and faster. Because teams invite ownership, they provide a mechanism for permanent monitoring and corrective action when a problem reappears. Team interaction develops creativity and innovation and the motivation needed to sustain team effort, effectiveness, and empowerment. Team success is never an accident. Remember, it is always the result of your intelligent effort, planning, and the necessary up-front training you give your staff. Team training can never be underestimated because your returns on this strategy will bring your school district benefits and profitability for years to come. Keep in mind, training is not just *important* to team success in your district; it is *necessary*.

SHARED DECISION MAKING

> Shared decision making satisfies team members' needs for belonging and power.

Next in your venture to implement teams, concentrate on fostering vision building. Shared decision making is the alternate leadership behavior to control and is nonbureaucratic in functioning. By empowering your staff, you are multiplying the points at which action can be initiated. Staff empowerment increases personal autonomy in team decisions of preference, choice, and judgment. It also increases innovation everywhere in the school. Through empowerment, initiative and choice are moved away from central administration. By empowering your staff, you are trading off some control to get more control. In other words, empowerment maximizes the opportunity for a new staff leadership. You can always go back to your old way of doing things; but resolve that if what you are doing is not working, you will be willing to change it.

The teaming process supports shared decision making in that it satisfies members' needs for belonging and power, thus focusing on their intrinsic motivations. Two motivational rules emerge through the group process:

- What is rewarding gets done.
- What we believe in and feel obligated to do gets done.

This is an important fact to remember—most staff members don't want to run the school. They want to be consulted on decisions that are going to affect them. Once they know what to expect, they usually will maintain the power balance between conformity and autonomy. Well-defined decision procedures are a must. Ideally, the team should discuss how decisions will be made, and, most important, data should be used as the basis for all decisions.

Participation and leadership must be distributed among members. All should participate and all should be listened to. As leadership needs arise, staff members should all feel responsible for meeting them. Through encouraging active staff participation in teams, the leader makes certain that all members are involved in problem solving, decision making, and implementation of the group's decisions to bring about satisfaction with their team membership.

When a process such as teaming makes people feel that they have a voice in matters that affect them, they will have greater commitment to the overall team efforts and will take greater responsibility for what happens as the outcome of their input. Shared decision making has been found to increase staff satisfaction, professionalism, and self-esteem; improve staff morale and efficiency; and help attract and retain quality personnel in our schools.

You must be willing to involve your staff in making decisions about the direction that educational improvements will take in your district. An able leader actively involves staff members in this type of leadership. What staff members need from their work is to be involved, to be accountable, and to reach for their potential, first as individual team members, then as successful district teams.

In schools, the leader's function ultimately becomes one of creating a community of shared values. The role of a leader in education must be changed to that of a leader of leaders, rather than a leader of followers. Specifically, you as the educational leader will need to develop skills of coach, partner, and cheerleader, if necessary. At times you may need to employ all these proficiencies in a given situation. Keep in mind, you have the power!

While having adequate resources can be helpful in initiating change, the starting point for school improvement can be simply a shift of attitude or point of view, first from you as the leader. For change to occur, you must first believe that change is necessary and possible through simple and practical methods. Leadership emerges from competence, and this belief in one's own abilities emerges from successful leadership. Your skill as a leader is nurtured when competence in your teams is first permitted and then further developed in shared team decision making. A new balance of power is created, a balance orchestrated by you and your vision for the future, by fostering collaborative effort in teams. A new team leadership is created under your watchful eye and the parameters you have set. Always remember you are the captain at the helm of your ship.

CHAPTER 3

Dimensions of Teams

TEAMING ADVANTAGES

While there are some obstacles to using teams (see table 3.1), there are more benefits when the teams are used correctly, such as the following:

- A team's early process improvements can convince school board members that progress is being made in increased short-term profitability.
- Teams can help convince members of the organization that the leadership is serious about quality improvements.
- Teams bring together diverse knowledge and skills.
- Teams encourage cooperation between different departments of an organization.
- Teams communicate the need for improvement and the status of improvement efforts.
- Teams can learn many aspects of continuous improvement through consensus and skills such as team building and group dynamics.
- Teams form closer links between professional staff development and student learning outcomes.

Teams can build a foundation for changing the culture of your educational organization. Teams grow stronger as the members recognize and acknowledge each other's strengths and foibles. This is the beginning of letting down one's defenses and paving the way toward thinking and acting as a team. With the cooperation of all team members, things are accomplished in a way that they could never have been before when attempted by individuals working independently.

Teams promote many organizational values by focusing on issues

Table 3.1 Working on teams.

Advantages	Disadvantages
Diverse knowledge and skills ⇒	Commitment of time and resources ⇐
Cooperation across departments ⇒	Following suggestions with alternatives not considered ⇐
Communication of improvement effort ⇒	Not supporting team decisions with actions ⇐

concerning education's internal and external clients. By their very existence they communicate the commitment of the organization to improving relationships. Teams form the basis for monitoring and adjusting processes, policies, and procedures. In a broad sense, teams in your district can improve communication, encourage cooperation, and further promote organizational quality improvements.

Teaming requires cross-functional membership in order to be successful. Teaming is a self-generative and organizationally generative activity. It is a process that induces continual improvement in the attitudes and behaviors toward self-management and organizational management. It also stimulates constructive changes in beliefs about self-efficiency and organizational improvement.

Understanding the school culture is a "knock on the door" of transformative educational change; changing that culture through team processes is the "key that will unlock the door" to continuous improvement action and lasting change efforts in our schools.

A cross-functional project team is a group consisting of members of different departments in an organization; persons with different roles who come together for problem solving and shared decision making, such as administrators, teachers, parents, students, secretaries, custodians, community members, and business leaders. The amount of time a project might otherwise take to complete can be reduced if the team consists of representatives of the areas critical to the project's completion. If a team solves problems, sets policies or goals, or comes up with ideas to improve the organization, all the departments represented also feel they have contributed to the organization's success. That, in turn, can boost morale throughout the entire organization. These project teams also assure that all departments get some voice in the solution, thereby avoiding the mind-set that they had no input into the solution and have to suffer the consequences.

A cross-functional project team can present opportunities for each team member to show leadership skills. One member might emerge as an organizational leader, an expert at figuring out what needs doing and who can round up the resources and get everyone pulling in the right direction. Another team member might be a visionary; he or she will do best at brainstorming sessions, coming up with ideas that are two or three steps ahead of everyone else's. Yet another team member might be a diplomat, the expert at nipping squabbles in the bud and keeping everyone feeling positive. As the work progresses, a pattern of distributed leadership forms. This distribution of skills will differ in each new team and will be as unique as the individual team members are themselves.

The way in which teams facilitate improvement may not always be obvious. It is not just through the methodical creation of procedures and actions that a team can be effective and efficient. The team also sets up education activities for all members. Nothing is more important than that. Teams provide the forum for active participation of staff members by seeking and incorporating their knowledge, understanding, and skills in a way that only they can. Real team learning comes from the experiences that the team members themselves have orchestrated with member input. For example, the purpose of childhood athletic teams is to help individuals learn more about getting along with others while understanding themselves better. Comprehension of life is the purpose. People who spend time on teams—athletic or organizational—will grow in their value to themselves as well as to the organization.

In the United States, the organizational model featuring narrow, functional middle managers operating within a rigid vertical and functional alignment is rapidly becoming obsolete. Organizations can now benefit from a structure that features suppliers, clients, and educational staff from different specialties crossing functional barriers and moving horizontally throughout the organization. If educational organizations are to respond to societal pressures, organizational members must change the way they think about education and its existing systems and structures. Cross-functional communication, coordination, and realignment are critical components of this new way of thinking.

Cross-functional teams need to become a major part of the new organizational structure in education. When guided properly, these project teams can provide the flexibility, multifunctional knowledge, and coordination mechanisms for fast responses to society's expectations and demands. Responses are required that traditional systems and structures in education cannot achieve. Remember, educational leaders cannot expect new outcomes from old inputs.

TEAMING DISADVANTAGES

When individuals form into groups, something always seems to get in the way of efficient progress. The problem is that there are hidden concerns and underlying tendencies that pull team members away from their obvious tasks. When team members walk into their meeting room, they encounter conflicting emotions. They feel both worried and excited about being on the team. As they anticipate the project's success, they are concerned that they stay loyal to their departments. If these undercurrents are left unattended, a team's success will be compromised.

Every team must spend the time needed to build support, respect, trust, and understanding within the group. Team issues that are not often discussed but are shared by many team members are as follows.

Are team members listening to one another? Listening is something we do every day. *Not* listening is something we do every day also. Real listening goes further than just passively receiving what someone else is saying. Use this strategy when real listening is necessary in a team situation: *Listen, Question, Restate.* A good listener can use this technique to help a speaker make a point and ensure everyone present understands it. Try it. It really can clarify issues.

Are team members open with one another? One hindrance to openness is the "hidden agenda"—a personal reason for trying to manipulate a meeting in one direction or another. There will be no hidden agendas if every team member makes the commitment to be honest while participating on the team. If you follow this strategy, you will create win-win situations.

Do team members trust one another? Underlying the team approach to decision making is the concept of *trust development*—a gradual building of trust among members of a team. The meeting environment should encourage this to happen. With a conscious effort by team members, a spirit of respect and trust will prevail at team meetings. You must keep in mind that it takes time for members to build trust among one another.

Every attempt by a team to improve your school district is an attempt to overcome obstacles. School districts are not institutions that wait passively to be changed. When it comes to building teams, there are some problems that must be overcome. Knowledge and understanding of these elements and circumstances will circumvent obstacles to a team's effectiveness. They have to do with several factors:

- Societal factors: More immediate issues are considered first; team building is not always of paramount concern.
- Budgets: Team building costs extra money; adequate resources are required.
- Unions: Union leadership is concerned about implications for teachers.
- Staff's knowledge: Team building is not alchemy; staff development is necessary.
- Team functioning: Communication of ideas is crucial for initiation of change.
- School schedules: Time must be built into the school schedule for team building.
- Continuity of staff: A measure of commitment is required by teams and district leadership.

The major problem that educational leaders face at some time or another in the implementation of the teaming process is the possibility that staff members decline the invitation to participate in problem solving and shared decision making. Not only is teacher resistance an issue in pursuing a collaborative, shared decision-making environment in our schools, but so is resistance by other staff members. People's unwillingness to implement policies after team decisions were made is another factor that limits the effectiveness of shared decision making in teams.

Though severe problems are rare, once the teaming process is in place, occasionally an individual member's behavior disrupts the group. Scholtes (1994) points out ten common group problems:

1. Floundering
2. Overbearing participants
3. Dominating participants
4. Reluctant participants
5. Unquestioned acceptance of opinion as facts
6. Rush to accomplishment
7. Attribution
8. Discounts and "plops"
9. Wanderlust: digression and tangents
10. Feuding members

The cross-functional project team concept is simple in theory, but the practical implementation of the team process is often difficult. Most educational organizations must overcome years of established practices and formal reporting structures. Integration of the use of teams requires an organizational culture of participative teamwork throughout all levels and across defined functional boundaries. The need to develop teamwork and cooperation is a major challenge in all organizations, not only in educational ones.

When teams are formed and members get to the business of teaming, sometimes more than the project at hand occupies their energies. Personal issues can be at the root of why some teams fail in their mission. It is ludicrous to think that just because a group of individuals formed a team to solve a problem that everyone will work cooperatively. You must guide the team as the ever-watchful leader, coach, and cheerleader.

THE POWER OF TEAMS

The power of teams is collective wisdom and effort.

The advantages of cross-functional project teams outweigh the disadvantages. Teaming in education takes time to evolve and gain recognition and acceptance, not only as a strategic process that can be achieved, but also as one that must be sought after. Teams can participate in the creation of a new and improved educational system that will become the catalyst that keeps our schools intellectually challenged and competitive.

Analysis of team advantages and disadvantages indicates that there is a limited amount of information on cross-functional project teams in service organizations, including education, while there is a large amount of literature and research on this teaming process in business and industry. However, the value of teamwork is slowly growing in recognition and acceptance as a highly efficient and effective process for problem solving and shared decision making in educational organizations.

Fostering collaborative efforts and strengthening the commitment of others to active involvement are crucial to revitalize education. Quality teams in education will become change agents if all organizational levels are involved in the process. Working together in teams encourages staff empowerment, creates a sense of ownership, and produces responsiveness to the pursuit of continuous improvement in educational services. Team building shapes the staff's leadership abilities and fosters collaboration and shared decision making by providing various school groups with the power necessary to make a difference.

As an educational leader, you are ready to empower your staff through the implementation of teams only when you are convinced of your own personal and professional abilities. You must overcome the fear of relinquishing your authority, which is characteristic of a hierarchical educational system that no longer effectively meets the needs of the community it serves. You need to encourage your staff's professional development, use the staff's expertise, and provide feedback that is honest, specific, and shared without fear. The key to this type of direction is to believe in and act on this powerful thought: "Empower others and others will empower you."

The more people believe that they can influence and guide the organization, the greater the organizational effectiveness and member satisfaction. Shared power results in greater job satisfaction and improved performance throughout the organization. Effective educational leaders cannot do everything by themselves; you must empower staff members to help reach organizational goals. Power at various educational levels should be shared, delegated, and transferred with flexible guidelines. Doing so creates a cyclical effect: The more power you share with staff, the more power as a leader you possess.

When this balance of power is in place, positive attitudes and accepted norms can heighten team motivation. Effective team building will occur only when individual team members accept and work toward common goals. This commitment gives meaning to personal and collective endeavors and, in turn, gives new meaning to the word *motivation*. In recent years, many American corporations have discovered that the workers who find meaning in their work perform more effectively. Active involvement is not required at all times, but commitment must always govern team members' thoughts, attitudes, and actions in the pursuit of school improvement. This commitment is evident in team processes that flatten the organizational hierarchy, speed decision making, create greater accountability, and improve how your staff feels about themselves and the organization. You must empower, encourage, and inspire staff to develop the skills and courage needed to function with less structure, less control, and increasing changes in the pursuit of quality in education.

There is no recipe or quick-fix answer to improve your district's schools. This transformation will not occur overnight, but it must come. If change is truly to be achieved, it will require careful planning by you as an educational leader who is committed to shared decision making through the use of teams. The following premise should be remembered throughout your journey toward continuous improvement: Quality is everyone's job and cannot be delegated to others. Quality in education through the power of teams is a bold digression from the lone administrator making decisions for the good of all. Will you wholeheartedly accept the challenge of teams in your organization?

The pros outweigh the cons when considering the use of teams in your educational organization. Explore the power of teams in your school district for the results that you seek. Each district is unique in its wants and needs. Teams are the vehicles to bring you closer to your vision of the future in your school district.

Part Three

WHAT'S HAPPENING IN TEAMS?

CHAPTER 4

Current Team Efforts

The value of teamwork has been established in business, industry, and health organizations through proven results in improved processes and products. The limited amount of research and information on cross-functional teams in educational organizations formed the rationale and action plan to study cross-functional teams in education.

My recent work with quality teams in education (Smialek, 1996) focused on team process patterns to facilitate systems improvement in education. The purpose of the study was to develop guidelines for the implementation of cross-functional teams in education by identifying the characteristics of teams that participated in problem solving and shared decision making and by identifying any commonalities that may have existed among the various teams. Increased knowledge of effective teams whose goals are continuous improvement relative to larger organizational issues is currently relevant to educational leaders, school staff, parents, students, and school board and community members who recognize a need for change in their school districts.

Data on teams (see table 4.1) and their achieved processes and products (see table 4.2) attest to the fact that the teams studied varied in composition, achieved process and/or product, and years of implementing quality in the school districts. Recurrent themes (see table 4.3) list in descending order the team strengths and considerations for improvement (weaknesses).

Each district's teams' strengths and considerations for improvement are presented to give examples of what worked to bring about successful team outcomes. In addition to the positive aspects noted are included the weaknesses that the teams experienced so that these pit-

Table 4.1 Data on school district teams.

School district	1	2	3	4
Geographic location	Western PA	Western PA	Eastern PA	Eastern PA
Geographic makeup	Suburban	Suburban	Suburban	Suburban/Rural
Enrollment	2,716	7,500	1,810	3,266
Professional staff	158	455	117	224
Number of schools	5 Elementary (3) Middle (1) Senior high (1)	12 Elementary (7) Middle (3) Intermediate high (1) Senior high (1)	4 Elementary (2) Middle (1) Senior high (1)	5 Elementary (3) Middle (1) Senior high (1)
Teams studied	3	3	3	3
TEAM A	High school code of conduct team	Flunk busters student retention team	Quality kid core team	District facilities planning team
Grade level	9-12	K-5	K-3	K-8
Representative team members interviewed team leader (T.L.)	Guidance counselor Teacher (T.L.) H.S. librarian Attendance secretary	Psychologist Curriculum supervisor Reading specialist (T.L.) Instructional Support teacher	Principal (T.L.) Teacher Business Partner/ Community member Parent	Superintendent (T.L.) Board member/ Senior citizen/ Community member Teacher Parent
Members on team	15	10	6	6
TEAM B	Student placement team	District form cutters team	Building governance team	Spelling improvement team
Grade level	K-5	K-12	3-5	4-5
Representative team members interviewed team leader (T.L.)	Principal Guidance counselor Teacher (T.L.) Teacher	Facilities secretary Business secretary Personnel secretary Ass't superintendent's secretary	Principal (T.L.) Teacher Parent Community member Business partner	Principal (T.L.) Two learning support teachers Two homeroom teachers
Members on team	10	6	10	10
TEAM C	District strategic planning team	MC/SR communication team	Organizational structure team	Two building collaborative team
Grade levels	K-12	K-10	K-5	K-3
Representative team members interviewed team leader (T.L.)	Superintendent (T.L.) Teacher Parent Student Community member	On-campus school coordinator Psychologist Ass't supervisor of special ed. Teacher (T.L.)	Principal (T.L.) Community member Parent Teacher	Two principals (T.L.) One teacher from each building
Members on team	15	15	10	10
Years implementing total quality in district	2	6	4	4

Table 4.2   Teams' improved process or product.

	District 1	District 2	District 3	District 4
Team's achieved process and product				
Team A	High school student code of conduct 9-12 Code of conduct procedures and code of Conduct Manual	Flunk busters student retention K-5 Retention guidelines, extended school year, five- week summer program, developmental K (1/2 day) & set up program K (whole day)	Quality kid core team K-3 Incorporation of quality principles into existing school program, quality principles and processes scheduled into existing school programs	District facilities planning team K-8 Hired architect for feasibility study, studying options that provide best educational environment at best possible cost
Team B	Student placement team K-5 Efficient student placement processes, Student placement form	District form cutters team Efficient absence from duty procedures, abbreviated absence from duty Form	Building governance team 3-5 Established improved relationships among parents, teachers, students, and administrators; real dialogue among the group members	Spelling improvement team 4-5 Consistent spelling instruction procedures, individualized spelling program for all students
Team C	District strategic planning team K-12 Graduation requirements, school to work program	MC/SR communication team K-10 School/residential program, student/staff clarification of school/ residential rules, student/staff manual	Organizational structure team K-5 Formulated homework policy, developed after-school homework program (H.E.L.P.) 3-5	Two building collaborative team K-3 Collaboration procedures for parent/staff development program for parents

falls may be avoided in your future team endeavors. Be prepared for some eye-opening information.

TEAM STRENGTHS AND CONSIDERATIONS FOR IMPROVEMENT

District 1: Team Strengths

All elements of team success in this district are in the area of inter-personal relationship skills. These areas of success stem mainly from personal attributes and skills of team members. The team members worked well with one another due mainly to balanced participation. Consensus was easily established. Teams were encouraged to take risks, and members felt that they were respected and trusted by other team

Table 4.3   Team's recurrent themes.

	Data from quality empowerment survey for teams (QUEST) and team interview questionnaire (TIQ)
	--DESCENDING ORDER OF TEAM STRENGTHS--
1.	**Decision making and problem solving**
	• teams have balanced participation
	• decisions and solutions are fully discussed before being evaluated
2.	**Respect and trust**
	• teams are encouraged to take risks
	• teams are both respected and trusted by team members themselves, peers, and district administrators
3.	**Team communications**
	• team members talk openly about ideas and problems
	• team members actively listen to each other
	• conflicts are confronted quickly and solved
4.	**Teamwork**
	• team members work well with one another
	• teams are well organized and produce quality outputs
	• team processes are efficient and timely
5.	**Recognition**
	• team members are recognized for their time and efforts as members on a district team
6.	**Goal clarity**
	• teams understand and are committed to team goals
	• individual team member goals match team goals
7.	**Initiative and creativity**
	• new ideas are supported and encouraged in district teams
	--DESCENDING ORDER OF TEAM CONSIDERATIONS FOR IMPROVEMENT--
1.	**Organizational systems and structures**
	• team empowerment will be expanded by changing current district systems, structures, and school policies to include more time for the team process during the regularly scheduled school day and to provide true representation of groups to voice their own opinions on all district teams
2.	**Information**
	• team empowerment will be increased if more effective and efficient methods are used to inform staff of what is going on in the teams and in the school district
3.	**Resources**
	• team empowerment will be augmented through a district staff development program and/or consultant team building training

members, peers, and district administrators. Team communications were strong, and the members received both support and encouragement for new ideas for process and product improvement.

District 1 did not have a formal recognition program. Team members, however, perceived that they were recognized for their time and efforts through verbal and written acknowledgments and small tokens of appreciation (e.g., quality pens, certificates).

District 1: Team Considerations for Improvement

A need to improve technical and team-building skills in the form of more team staff development and/or consultant training was voiced by study participants. Another area of concern was to establish a better, more consistent method of keeping the staff informed of what is going on in teams throughout the district.

Team members believed that increased team empowerment would be ensured with the representation of essential client groups, namely parents and students, on an as-needed basis in district teams in order for them to voice their own concerns.

District 2: Team Strengths

Team communication was the highest-ranking, most successful element of team success in this district. Data suggests that team members talked openly about their ideas and problems. Team members actively listened to each other, and conflicts were quickly confronted and solved. The teams were well organized to produce a quality output; team processes were completed in an efficient and timely manner. A strong point of this district's teams is that individual team member goals matched team goals. Teams were respected and trusted. Their balanced participation and the follow-through of decisions and solutions after being fully discussed were other strong areas. Although this district does not have a formal recognition program, team members perceived that they were recognized for their time and efforts. At the end of the school year, the district's teams received their city's Excellence Council Team Award. Plaques were awarded at a banquet to a representative number of team members. Small tokens of appreciation were given at the district level throughout the school year. Support for team initiative and encouragement of individual initiative were also ranked as strengths of the teaming process in this district. A plus noted by team members was the strength of acquiring the necessary technical and team-building skills by way of staff development and consultant training. Team training was an important focus of all teams.

District 2: Team Considerations for Improvement

Keeping staff informed of what was going on in district teams was a concern of team members. Team members emphasized a need to have current system structures and current school policies changed to include teaming processes in the regularly scheduled school day. This requirement is vital to make teams work in education and to promote buy-in from staff. Expanded representation of essential groups, namely parents and students, in district teams to voice their own concerns would increase team effectiveness, as reported by team members surveyed.

District 3: Team Strengths

Respect and trust of administrators, peers, and team members ranked number one as the most successful element to this district's team successes. Team members were encouraged to take risks to produce a quality output in a teaming environment in which processes were efficient and timely. Team members received not only verbal and written recognition but monetary compensation also. Team communications were strong. A forum to speak openly about ideas, problems, and solutions was encouraged. In this atmosphere, team decision making and problem solving came in an easy manner, according to interviewed team members. Another real strength of this district was its commitment to balanced participation on all teams. All team members evaluated decisions and resolutions in each of the teams studied.

District 3: Team Considerations for Improvement

Team members strongly agreed there should be a district team initiative implemented in the area of promoting initiative and creativity. The team members surveyed and interviewed were all from one school in the district. Team members rated both team initiative and creativity in this particular school very high. The need for formal team training and districtwide staff development programs ranked extremely high. Team members in the study all had prior formal training or former professional training that was easily transferred to the necessary team-building skills to ensure team successes. (Three-fourths of the interviewed members fell into this category.) Interview data shows that one-half of the representative team members had, on the average, two days of team training. This technical training and team building was sponsored by the teams' business partnerships. There was indecisiveness as to whether the team process provided team members with opportunities for personal and career growth. Because these highly effective teams were from one building in the district, many of the same participants were on more than one team at the same time. To encourage districtwide team initiative, team members noted a genuine need to keep district staff well informed of teaming efforts.

District 4: Team Strengths

Team member interactions ranked number one with this district's team members. Data corroborates the fact that District 4 teams were well organized and members talked freely about their beliefs and opinions. Goal clarity was a powerful force. Team members were committed to team goals, and individual member goals matched team goals. In this district, all team members had the information needed to do their jobs. The data supports that both staff and parents were kept informed of what was going on in the districts' teams. Recognition was another successful attribute of all teams in the district. Although it has an individual staff member recognition program only, team members perceived that they were recognized for their time and efforts on teams, although no examples of team recognition were given in the interview data. Their continuous process and product improvement was due to a high ranking of initiative and creativity by team members. On the teams studied, necessary technical and interpersonal skills were present. Three-fourths of the members had prior formal team training and former professional development that were transferred to their teaming processes. A noted plus was the administrative support that was available to teams when needed.

District 4: Team Considerations for Improvement

True representation of essential groups on teams to voice their own concerns was an area of need. School board and community members, parents, and students need to be included on future teams. Two other areas of concern surfaced during the interview process: Over half of the interviewed team members stressed the need for team-building training on a district level through a staff development program. Also, the need for time for teaming processes scheduled during the school day was mentioned as a perceived need by almost half of the team members interviewed.

The results of this team study established commonsense guidelines to enable successful teaming patterns. These are as follows:

- Provide needed team-building training, including both technical skills and interpersonal relationship skills, in the form of district staff development programs or outside consultant training
- Include necessary time in the school schedule for the teaming processes
- Provide an environment that is receptive to team members' opinions and ideas as well as one that provides support and encouragement for new ideas and follows through on team recommendations
- Include on teams a true representation of all concerned groups in order for them to voice their own concerns as well as provide balanced participation to facilitate decision making and problem-solving outcomes
- Respect and trust team members
- Ensure effective and efficient methods of communication among team members, staff, administrators, parents, and community members
- Recognize team members for their time and efforts

These guidelines can be translated into the seven steps to team success.

SEVEN STEPS TO TEAM SUCCESS

The following seven steps to team success were deemed essential in considering team effectiveness and empowerment, according to the representative team members who were surveyed and interviewed. The steps are ranked in order of importance to team success.

Step 1. Team Training

Team training ranked as the most significant step and is regarded as the most necessary element of team effectiveness and success.

In interviews with team training consultants from business and training organizations (e.g., Shadyside Hospital, Pittsburgh, Pa.; Joiner Associates, Madison, Wis.; American Society for Quality Control, Milwaukee, Wis.; and Medrad Corporation, Pittsburgh, Pa.), the average team training in business and industry for team members is forty hours. Data analysis from this team study attests that teams in education receive much less training.

The issue of adequate training for teams is a consideration for improvement in all participating districts of the study. Staff training in the regular school schedule must be allowed in order to develop the necessary climate and a culture that values shared decision making in teams. Restructuring the school day is a prerequisite for this project. To provide release time for staff training, community members can assist by teaching the students a wide variety of information lifestyle skills (e.g., career planning, wellness issues, special interests). Staff must be trained to work smarter, but they need the time to do it. Providing training on scheduled early dismissal days or staff development days is an option; these times are alternatives for goal-oriented discussions and training for all staff.

Step 2. Time

The second major step for team success was the issue of time in the regularly scheduled school day. In the districts, team meetings were held before and after school, with some evening team meetings. Team members mentioned that they had release time for team meetings during the regularly scheduled school day occasionally but not in any consistent manner or scheduled time slot. This release time could be expanded to encompass team meetings during the regular school day with the aid of substitute teachers and/or community volunteers. School schedules could be developed that incorporate time for the teaming process built right into the regularly scheduled school day.

Step 3. True Representation of Groups

True representation of groups was the third major issue cited by team members to ensure team success. Accordingly, practitioners should give serious consideration to the nature of their education partners. Educators must make every effort to solicit the multiple voices of students, parents, and school board and community members and to let them define their own version of quality, rather than allowing others who hold more power to speak for them.

Step 4. Follow-through on Team Recommendations

The step ranked fourth by the team members was following through on team recommendations. This follow-through on team actions and solutions is a perceived necessary element of successful and empowered teams. Team members, on various district teams, mentioned in the interviews how disheartening to team members and how detrimental to the teaming process it was to have team recommendations changed by an administrator. It is a real waste of the team members' time if team recommendations are not followed through. Implications for district administrators would be to honor team recommendations or forgo the teaming process altogether and make decisions at the administrative level in the first place.

Before rushing into full acceptance and implementation of teams in education, address the predominant issue of goals. To what degree is the school district oriented toward regulation or educational change? The goal continuum will shape all other aspects of the quality process of continuous improvement. That is, the goals will determine who is invited to participate in problem solving and shared decision making and how those persons are empowered to participate. The implication is that team participants should be selected based not only on hierarchical position (e.g., administrators, teachers, business leaders, community members, parents, and students) but also on social function position (e.g., teachers of students with disabilities, economically poor students, parents of students of color, working-class community members, and senior citizens on fixed incomes).

Step 5. Respect and Trust

The fifth major step to team success is the element of respect and trust regarding openness to team members' opinions.

Respect and trust are the cornerstones of educational innovation in our schools. Future educational leaders need to go beyond *you* ("you do this and that"), or dependence, to *I*, which is independence, and eventually to *we*, or interdependence. Leaders in education in the new paradigm of learning are at the *we* level where responsibility is shared; both the victories and the defeats are shared and synergy is nurtured.

According to Senge (1990), "The child learns school is not about learning; it's about performing and not making mistakes." The same is true for educational organizations that want to change; all learning involves making mistakes. How can an organization learn if all its procedures and systems are about avoiding mistakes? To institute lasting change, school systems and individuals must learn to challenge existing mental models of education. Some of the fundamental assumptions—for example, that staff and students don't want to learn and must be motivated, that learning is about requiring information, and that there are right answers and wrong answers—must be challenged by educational leaders. We have to maintain openness, a willingness to continually reflect on these assumptions. That is the real challenge in creating an educational system for all its members. The informants in all four school districts stressed openness and communication maintenance as necessary components to ensure team empowerment.

Step 6. Information

The sixth step to team success is the element of needed information. Data analyzed included both the surveyed and interviewed team members. Team empowerment is increased as perceived by the representative team members if more effective and efficient methods are used to inform team members, staff, administrators, parents, and community members of what is going on in the teams and in the school district. In order to implement this, an option would be to poll district members as to what method of information dissemination would best suit both individual and district needs.

Step 7. Recognition

The issue of team recognition, the seventh step to team success, while not a significant area of concern at this time, was, however, an area of noted importance for the commitment to future team endeavors. The synergy that comes from team members working together productively on an improvement project is usually enough to sustain their enthusiasm and support them through difficult times and hectic schedules in the short term. To sustain empowered teaming processes, educational organizational changes must reflect shared power, shared responsibilities, and shared rewards.

A northern suburban school district of Pittsburgh set aside mini-grants for summer team training. An action team was set up to survey staff as to what types of rewards should be given for team participation. Suggested rewards included compensation time, release time from duties with substitutes covering them, breakfast or lunch meetings, and recognition in districtwide publications.

Future considerations for increased team member recognition include the following:

- Establishing release time for team members to complete in-depth team training
- Applying for corporate "gifts" from business partnerships
- Developing staff team-training courses, including quality principles and practices
- Applying to the Foundation for Excellence for employee incentive grants
- Establishing career pathways for trainers and facilitators

- Developing a cadre of trained team facilitators and trainers
- Using additional hours in contract for just-in-time training

OVERVIEW OF TEAM PROCESSES

In all of the participating school district teams studied, team members decided what was to be done and how it was to be done within the parameters imposed by the larger goals of their educational organizations. The work of teams was challenging and fulfilling to the team members themselves. Resistance to change was lessened as a result of a broader base of educational leadership in each of the districts when ownership of the process of improvement was delegated to the team members. Team members agreed that under these new directions in educational leadership, expanded preparation and training of staff are necessary so that school personnel may acquire and develop the knowledge base and interpersonal and technical skills necessary to continue on the journey of continuous educational improvement in teams. A minimal amount of team training was given to the teams that were studied. This expanded comprehensive team training was not evident in any of the school districts. All teams studied were viable entities effecting change in their school districts with the support of a progressive and visionary educational leadership, but they functioned without all of the necessary elements to create real team empowerment. The teaming process in education was being implemented in the researched school districts but on a limited basis due to the lack of organizational systems and structures necessary to support team efficiency and true empowerment.

The real challenge for future educational leaders is to be aware of the seven steps to team success presented in this study and to "set the stage" for team empowerment by assuring that all of these elements are accounted for and provided to ensure a most effective team process. Team empowerment is not an arbitrary process. It must be orchestrated by open and supportive leaders who will ensure that the necessary organizational systems and structures (e.g., technical and interpersonal skills training, time in the school schedule, needed information, and resources) are available to support the team process in their school districts.

The team members who were surveyed and interviewed were committed, hardworking individuals. They emphasized that their teams were successful in that their goals were met, but not without problems. According to team members, the following educational organizational systems and structures (in descending order) were not always available when needed: team training, time for the team process, follow-through on team recommendations, and true representation of groups on teams to voice their own concerns. The issue of follow-through on team recommendations appears to be a particular problem only in educational organizations. That educational leaders did not follow through on team recommendations was a noted concern of team members in each of the researched school districts. This was the only concern of team members that was not cited in a review of related cross-functional team literature in business and industry. Team members raised the question of sustained administrative commitment. Future educational leaders must address the predominant issue of their goals before the acceptance and implementation of the teaming process in their school districts. Teaming processes will not be successful if commitment to them is on a superficial basis.

Effective strategies extending beyond the boundaries of traditional education are necessary to provide the level of educational experiences required in the future. Educational leaders must be open-minded about educational redesign through the teaming process. Employing the team empowerment model for education (see chapter 6) will require that ideas not be constrained by the limitations of what can easily be done within the current educational system and structure in your district. Exploring new possibilities for designing the future of education in teams will surely bring about greater effectiveness and efficiency in education. Reading the given background information on teams in education and their current progress in some school districts, I'm sure you are thinking, What must I do first to begin a rewarding team initiative in my district? Help is just a page away.

Part Four

BUILDING SUCCESSFUL TEAMS

CHAPTER 5

Simple and Easy Strategies That Work

TEN STEPS TO GETTING A NEW TEAM STARTED

The team process usually begins with the superintendent and an administrative steering committee creating an initial pilot project team. In my work with teams (Smialek, 1996), some principals took on this role in their own schools and were quite successful in their endeavors. The administrative steering committee, either at the district level or building level, generally will choose several issues for teams to address. This committee also establishes guidelines and the all-important timetables for results. It is also the job of the steering committee to provide any resources the team will need. Another important consideration at this juncture is to be sure that the team members' goals are aligned with the district goals.

The following ten steps are helpful in getting a new team started. Use the following outline as a checklist to increase your team's successful outcomes in your district.

1. Select project to be addressed
2. Select representative team members
3. Set goals:
    a. Include long-term objectives (statement of purpose)
    b. Itemize short-term procedures (plan for completion)
    c. Develop a mission statement
       • Clarify focus of project
       • Set boundaries
       • Develop a schedule
4. Focus on clients:
    a. Determine who they are
    b. Clarify clients' expectations

5. Focus on work processes:
   a. Note improvement opportunities
   b. Gather data
   c. Analyze data (separate observation from inference)
6. Conduct productive meetings:
   a. Use an agenda
   b. Employ team meeting roles:
      • Facilitator
      • Timekeeper
      • Scribe (writes documentation during meeting for members)
      • Note taker (prepares minutes)
   c. Draft agenda for next meeting
   d. Summarize decisions made
   e. Gain consensus on action plans
   f. Evaluate meeting:
      • Discuss what went well
      • Note improvements that should be considered
      • Communicate meeting conclusions to others
7. Carry out proposed assignments
8. Document team's progress
   a. Choose effective methods of communication
9. Initiate project closure
   a. Evaluate project completion
   b. Maintain process improvement supported by organizational systems and structures
10. Celebrate project completion
    a. Recognize team's efforts
    b. Choose appropriate ways to mark team success:
       • Bestow small tokens of appreciation
       • Share breakfast/lunch/dinner
       • Write comments
       • Provide awards/certificates
       • Give monetary compensation

FACILITATING TEAM PROCESSES

You are proud of your efforts so far in initiating team processes in your district. You put together your first team and it is sailing! Let's call it Team A.

You've internalized the information set forth in this book. You've accepted the challenge of teams in your district. You've considered the necessary components of the right team environment. You've thoroughly reviewed team advantages as well as team disadvantages in your district. You, too, were encouraged about current team efforts and successes in other districts.

But now, after so much hard work and motivation, your personal momentum is waning. Your team, which was so enthusiastic, is almost at a standstill. Team members sense all is not well. You and your team are not quite sure which direction to go.

In this type of situation, or a similar one, try a simple and easy strategy that works. First, consider this scenario:

Team A has a dilemma. It can't pinpoint why it is faltering. Its vision has been set and its mission is defined. Key processes have been mapped. Statistical process controls have been employed. Methods for measuring team performance have been developed. Team members thought they had all the bases covered, yet the team's level of productivity and performance is still questionable. The group doesn't know why, how, or where to begin to get back on track. Team members don't believe that optimal performance is achievable for their team, and they have not been able to pinpoint the team's strengths and weaknesses. What should the team do next?

When looking for a solution to team problems, it is important to remember that every team is different. No one method will jump-start and adequately serve every team in every way. Teams are different in physical, technical, educational, and training makeup. Each team must find its own recipe for success.

To maximize team performance, each team must know and capitalize on its strengths and overcome its weaknesses. Simply wanting better team performance is not enough to create a successful team. How can teams focus on their efforts and desired results so that all members can recognize their contributions?

Constant improvement, innovation, and integration of quality are needed at all organizational levels for all teams. This is the key to the team's long-term plan for success. The question is, How does a team arrive at a successful conclusion in a reasonable length of time? A resource is needed to help identify critical issues and weave solutions into the team's structure. The sooner the team's needs are addressed, the sooner the team will succeed.

THE QUEST SOLUTION: A DIAGNOSTIC/ PRESCRIPTIVE TOOL

The Quality Empowerment Survey for Teams (QUEST) shown in figure 5.1 is a resource designed to help teams pinpoint challenges to success and capitalize on both individual member and team strengths. The QUEST will clarify and remedy any areas impeding team success. The key to this diagnostic tool is that it is easy to use and interpret (see table 5.1). In a matter of minutes individual member and team strengths and weaknesses are evident. With this information each area of concern can be broken into root causes that need corrective action.

All organizations—whether health care, educational, or business—can benefit from the diagnostic and prescriptive properties of the QUEST to help identify individual and team strengths as well as the blind spots inhibiting team empowerment. It can help a team expand its knowledge and understanding of team interaction and effectiveness by fostering the skills, strategies, and techniques needed to achieve team empowerment. Without the skills, abilities, and knowledge that such a resource can generate, teams can remain stifled and unable to successfully tackle problems and reach higher levels of performance. With growing frequency, the team's successes will prove that principles such as focusing on customers, using data effectively, improving processes, and working cooperatively are no longer just buzzwords; they are fundamental to creating more effective organizations.

When trying to turn a team around, the challenges to leaders and facilitators are not always obvious. Identifying the team's strengths and weaknesses and taking the time to analyze them will maximize the team's success.

ANALYSIS AND INTERPRETATION

Once the team's strengths and weaknesses are known, the results can be analyzed and interpreted with the information in figure 5.2. How can the team use this information to improve its efficiency and effectiveness? An educational rule of thumb is to overcome the team's weaknesses by employing its strengths to achieve that goal. In figure 5.2, Team A's strengths, which include supporting and encouraging new ideas (strength no. 1) and confronting and solving conflicts quickly (strength no. 2) and efficiently (strength no. 3), can and should be used to remediate the team's weaknesses.

Analyzing Team A's weaknesses shows that team members do not actively listen to one another (weakness no. 1). This is a major failing

---

QUALITY
EMPOWERMENT
SURVEY
FOR
TEAMS
(QUEST)©

INTRODUCTION

How empowered is your team? How empowered are you as an individual team member? Measure and analyze your team's strengths and your own individual strengths as a team member. Gather information for planning and monitoring purposes to enhance shared decision making.

SURVEY INFORMATION
Name:_____
Role on team:_____
Team goal:_____
Personal goal for being on this team:_____
_____
_____
_____

DIRECTIONS
After each statement, please indicate your response by circling the appropriate number; add numbers for each section; and record total in appropriate box.

Strongly Agree (SA)
Agree (A)
Disagree (D)
Strongly Disagree (SD)
Undecided (U)

Figure 5.1   *Quality empowerment survey for teams (QUEST).*

QUEST

1.	**RESPECT AND TRUST**	SA	A	D	SD	U	
(a)	I feel respected by team members	1	2	3	4	5	
(b)	Team members trust each other.	1	2	3	4	5	
(c)	Our team is trusted by its peers.	1	2	3	4	5	
(d)	Our team is respected by management.	1	2	3	4	5	
(e)	I am encouraged to take risks.	1	2	3	4	5	
	TOTAL SCORE						
2.	**RECOGNITION**	SA	A	D	SD	U	
(a)	I am recognized for my contributions to our team.	1	2	3	4	5	
(b)	Our team expects the best from each member.	1	2	3	4	5	
(c)	Management recognizes individual efforts.	1	2	3	4	5	
(d)	Management recognizes team efforts.	1	2	3	4	5	
(e)	Our organization recognizes people for their ability not for who they know.	1	2	3	4	5	
	TOTAL SCORE						
3.	**TEAM COMMUNICATIONS**	SA	A	D	SD	U	
(a)	Team members talk openly about ideas.	1	2	3	4	5	
(b)	Team members talk openly about problems.	1	2	3	4	5	
(c)	Team members actively listen to each other.	1	2	3	4	5	
(d)	The team regularly communicates with management.	1	2	3	4	5	
(e)	Conflicts are confronted quickly and solved.	1	2	3	4	5	
	TOTAL SCORE						
4.	**INFORMATION**	SA	A	D	SD	U	
(a)	I have all information needed to do my job.	1	2	3	4	5	
(b)	Our team has all needed information to do its job.	1	2	3	4	5	
(c)	Individuals are kept informed of what is going on in the team.	1	2	3	4	5	
(d)	Individuals are kept informed of what is going on in the organization.	1	2	3	4	5	
(e)	Our team knows how to get needed information.	1	2	3	4	5	
	TOTAL SCORE						

Figure 5.1   *(Continued)*

5.	**DECISION MAKING AND PROBLEM SOLVING**	SA	A	D	SD	U	
(a)	Members are encouraged to speak out.	1	2	3	4	5	
(b)	Adequate time is spent searching for innovative solutions.	1	2	3	4	5	
(c)	Members use win/win techniques.	1	2	3	4	5	
(d)	Decisions are not evaluated without being fully discussed.	1	2	3	4	5	
(e)	Solutions are not evaluated without being fully discussed.	1	2	3	4	5	
	TOTAL SCORE						
6.	**RESOURCES**	SA	A	D	SD	U	
(a)	Our team receives needed resources on time.	1	2	3	4	5	
(b)	The members of our team have all the necessary technical skills.	1	2	3	4	5	
(c)	The members of our team have all the necessary team skills.	1	2	3	4	5	
(d)	Priorities are consistently clear.	1	2	3	4	5	
(e)	Management support is clearly available when needed.	1	2	3	4	5	
	TOTAL SCORE						
7.	**INITIATIVE AND CREATIVITY**	SA	A	D	SD	U	
(a)	Our team has full support for taking initiative.	1	2	3	4	5	
(b)	Individual initiative is encouraged by our team.	1	2	3	4	5	
(c)	Team initiative is encouraged by the organization.	1	2	3	4	5	
(d)	It is easy for our team to suggest new ideas for improving processes and products.	1	2	3	4	5	
(e)	It is easy for the team to try new ideas for improving processes and products.	1	2	3	4	5	
	TOTAL SCORE						
8.	**GOAL CLARITY**	SA	A	D	SD	U	
(a)	Our team knows/understands the team's goals.	1	2	3	4	5	
(b)	Our team is committed to the team's goals.	1	2	3	4	5	
(c)	My individual goals match the team's goals.	1	2	3	4	5	
(d)	Our team allows me the opportunity for personal growth.	1	2	3	4	5	
(e)	Our team allows me the opportunity for career growth.	1	2	3	4	5	
	TOTAL SCORE						

Figure 5.1   (Continued)

PAGE 3 OF 3						
9.	**TEAMWORK**	SA	A	D	SD	U
(a)	Individuals on our team work well together to solve difficult problems.	1	2	3	4	5
(b)	Individuals on our team focus on the team not themselves.	1	2	3	4	5
(c)	Our team does not focus around one or two "superstars."	1	2	3	4	5
(d)	We are well organized to produce a quality output.	1	2	3	4	5
(e)	Our team processes are efficient (and timely).	1	2	3	4	5
	TOTAL SCORE					
10.	**ORGANIZATIONAL SYSTEMS AND STRUCTURES**	SA	A	D	SD	U
(a)	Organizational policies are consistent with team goals.	1	2	3	4	5
(b)	Our team easily interacts with other teams in our organization.	1	2	3	4	5
(c)	Team empowerment in our organization can happen without changing major systems and structures.	1	2	3	4	5
(d)	Our team can be empowered without changing current systems and structures.	1	2	3	4	5
(e)	Our team can be empowered without changing current organization policies.	1	2	3	4	5
	TOTAL SCORE					

Figure 5.1   (Continued)

of this team because effective listening is not only one of the most important methods for acquiring knowledge and for problem solving, it can also be the hardest and most active work any team member is called upon to do. If team members don't actively listen, decisions and solutions cannot be fully discussed (weakness no. 2). This breakdown leads to an underlying problem of Team A, which is that team member goals do not match team goals (weakness no. 3). This indicates that the member makeup of Team A is not suitable to effectively make decisions and solve problems that are consistent with achieving the team's goals.

During this stage of the team's analysis, it may be necessary to secure a more appropriate member representation on the team to carry out the team's goals, or perhaps it may be necessary to monitor or adjust the team's goals while maintaining original members. Again, the team's strengths listed in figure 5.2 support the latter solution because the strengths of the team members are able to support these new changes for the better. Revised or changed goals would probably be

Table 5.1   Interpreting your QUEST scores.

Enter below your individual total and average each of the ten empowerment factors. Circle the three that have the highest average.   Next, when the team gets back together, add your individual totals for each factor to the totals of the others on your team.   Then determine the team's average for each of the factors.   Place an asterisk next to the three empowerment factors which had the highest totals for the team.

		YOUR TOTAL	YOUR AVERAGE	TEAM AVERAGE	TEAM RANGE
1.	RESPECT AND TRUST				
2.	RECOGNITION				
3.	TEAM COMMUNICATIONS				
4.	INFORMATION				
5.	DECISION MAKING AND PROBLEM SOLVING				
6.	RESOURCES				
7.	INITIATIVE AND CREATIVITY				
8.	VISION/GOAL CLARITY				
9.	TEAMWORK				
10.	ORGANIZATION SYSTEMS AND STRUCTURE				

The team should be concerned with any team average that is over 2.0.   Your team discussion should begin with the three highest team average scores. The team should also look at factors where the range between the lowest and the highest score is greater than one. This indicates a divergence of how team members perceive the situation and environment. Finally, if any of your individual averages were higher than 2.0 and are not covered in the discussion of team factors, you should raise those issues with the team.

When discussing a factor, it is helpful to talk about each of the subpoints individually. The discussion should lead the team to the factors which need improvement in order for the team to become more empowered.   Break each factor into the root causes which need corrective action.

Create a plan for improvement.

accepted by Team A since, according to figure 5.2, new ideas are supported and encouraged (strength no. 1), conflicts are confronted quickly and solved (strength no. 2), and projected team outcomes are timely and efficient (strength no. 3).

A thorough analysis encompassing all strengths and weaknesses of Team A is presented here, but other team analyses need not be as detailed. By reflecting on the team's strengths and weaknesses, team leaders, facilitators, and even team members can come to the means of

- In one column, write the team's strengths.
- See if the differences between the sides are important for the team's work and successful outcomes. If yes, develop a plan for getting information that will help resolve the issues.

STRENGTHS	CONSIDERATIONS
New ideas are supported and encouraged.	Team members do not actively listen to one another.
Conflicts are confronted quickly and solved.	Decisions and solutions are not fully discussed.
Team processes are timely and encouraged.	Team member goals do not match team goals.

Figure 5.2 *Team strengths and considerations for improvement.*

change for the better for the team. If the team doesn't feel comfortable employing a detailed analysis like the one presented, then it should start by focusing on just one of the team's weaknesses. First, the team should ask the question "Why?" When this question is successfully answered, it should ask the same question again. Inadvertently, the team will come closer and closer to identifying the roadblock to its effectiveness. As the team becomes more comfortable with using the QUEST, team strengths and weaknesses will become easier to analyze.

The QUEST will provide results that enable the team to diagnose setbacks to its progress. What team members do with the results is up to them. The degree of analysis and interpretation of the team's survey results will depend on how, when, and where the team chooses to use them.

Employing the QUEST yields profit from a team's intellectual capital. It confirms the value of the team's power and focuses on areas that present a challenge. Using a resource such as the QUEST helps team leaders, members, and facilitators maximize a team's task and relationship energy when working on situations that demand change for the better. It is possible to tailor team efforts to fit each team's needs. A little time and effort will yield a great output in team results.

The tangible force of the QUEST is using a common tool to educate team leaders, facilitators, and team members so that all members can communicate in a common language. While pinpointing the strengths and weaknesses of the team, there will be no guessing as to the root causes of problems. The QUEST offers the methodology that allows the team to focus on problem-solving resources to achieve the desired results. The QUEST is a powerful tool that can help address the team's needs and help it reach its potential. Teams can work in education, and the QUEST is an effective method to help pinpoint challenges, capitalize on team strengths, and help teams work successfully.

The QUEST has not only been successfully used in school districts but has found a variety of applications. Most recently it has been tested successfully in businesses and health care organizations. The largest private-hospital management company in Germany, currently running fifty-two hospitals with 14,000 beds, has improved both processes and products within its organization by using this diagnostic/prescriptive tool. The QUEST was translated into the German language and the results are to be published in a German hospital management magazine. Also, the QUEST is currently being adapted for use in business to help improve international teaming processes between engineers in the United States and France who are working on a joint project.

The QUEST's use and application are universal. It is a direct, simple, and easy method to determine precisely where there is a breakdown in the teaming process so that remediation can take place to improve the quality of the work of teams in your school district.

CHAPTER 6

Team Empowerment:
How Do You Get It Right?

THE TEAM EMPOWERMENT MODEL FOR EDUCATION

To build a culture of continuous learning and improvement, an educational organization and its leaders need an action plan detailing steps to work toward team empowerment and a framework for applying them. The organization needs a system that will enable successes for teams. If you are willing and able to give teams a try in your district or learning organization, do what matters and what works in education.

While I was working with district teams and learning from their successes and their trials and errors, patterns emerged as to what, when, where, and how things need to be for teaming processes to be successful. By assuring that certain elements, individuals, resources, agencies, systems, and structures are in place at various levels within and about the organization, you can make team empowerment a reality for your organization.

The seven steps to team success in education (in chapter 4) form the action plan to guide educational leaders in facilitating continuous improvement in their educational systems. With these guidelines in place, everyone in the organization works systematically toward team empowerment. When you apply these seven steps, the following results:

- Everyone at their own organizational level has an increased power of action, strengthened with necessary skills and experiences in the teaming process.
- Everyone receives and shares needed information at the right time, in the right form.

- Everyone and every team activity is focused on continuous learning and growth.

The team empowerment model for education (see figure 6.1 and table 6.1) presents the following beneficial results:

- A strong and flexible conceptual architecture
- A proven application of elements based on the seven steps to team success in education

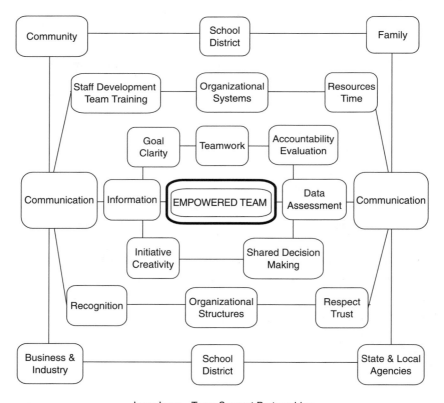

Inner Loop—Team Support Partnerships
Middle Loop—Internal District Support Partnerships
Outer Loop—External Client Support Partnerships

Figure 6.1 *Team empowerment model for education.*

Table 6.1 Overview of keys to team success.

	Keys to Team Member Support	**Relation to Team Empowerment**
	Inner Loop	
Key 1	Goal Clarity	Clear goals guide team improvement efforts.
Key 2	Initiative/Creativity	Creative initiative stimulates team activity and leads team closer to its goals.
Key 3	Teamwork	Synergy due to pooling of team member efforts sustains team endeavors.
Key 4	Information	Communication encourages cooperation that leads to suggestions for improvement.
Key 5	Data Assessment	Analysis of data provides a means to check effectiveness of actions to facilitate improvement efforts.
Key 6	Accountability/Evaluation	Team assessment keeps members focused and moving in the right direction.
Key 7	Shared Decision Making	Consensus forms the basis of successful team outcomes.
	Keys to Internal District Support	**Relation to Team Empowerment**
	Middle Loop	
Key 1	Respect/Trust	Respect/Trust form the cornerstone of innovation and substantive change.
Key 2	Team Training	Staff development generates the climate and culture that values shared decision making.
Key 3	Resources/Time	Resources maintain and facilitate team processes in continuous improvement.
Key 4	Recognition	Recognizing team members sustains empowered processes by shared rewards.
Key 5	Systems	Work processes should be designed to support organizational goals.
Key 6	Structures	Organization construction should foster continuous improvement processes.
	Keys to External Client Support	**Relation to Team Empowerment**
	Outer Loop	
Key 1	Family	Client satisfaction supports teaming processes. Collaboration with family determines student needs.
Key 2	Community	Informed choices are more accurate coupled with the skills and resources of community members.
Key 3	Agencies	Assisted technology and service experts facilitate relationships with suppliers and distributors to improve quality of services.
Key 4	Business/Industry	Technical direction and corroboration reduces cost, improves quality and cycle time for teaming processe

- An integrated whole framework
- Alignment of the various levels of the organization by creating necessary support partnerships
- A highly competitive and quality education system realized through the power of teaming processes

The team empowerment model for education's design supports the structural, interpersonal, external, and internal relationships governing the educational organization's operations.

This framework is a master checklist that ensures the proper plan of both strategy and structure and nurtures the development of a unified approach to guide your educational teaming processes. It is based on the premise that educational teams are composed of a number of inter-related processes that cannot be influenced independently of each other. These series of systematic actions and their coordination and linkage to the organization's strategic plans will result in continuous process and product improvement over time.

The components of the team empowerment model for education are as follows:

- Team support partnerships: The inner loop establishes the neces-sary elements for team members to function as an empowered team.
- Internal district support partnerships: The middle loop profiles the roles of the school district to ensure an environment for team empowerment.
- External client support partnerships: The outer loop defines the external representation of client groups to voice their own con-cerns. These partnerships provide the technical support and the resources needed to facilitate an improved educational system while ensuring client satisfaction.

These components have been highlighted to refine educational leaders' thinking about how to define, build, and empower their teams. To bring about successful teaming processes and to promote continuous improvement in education, these three distinct levels—the team itself, district leadership, and the clients of the school district—must form cooperative relationships. Successful educational organizations are aware of their existence and components and will organize their growth around them. Educational organizations that desire to foster educational change for the better through teams should employ all three support partnership components in a balanced, workable fashion. This will not only facilitate team processes at all levels of the organization, but will ensure successful district outcomes. All concerned clients of education will have their forum along with the district's support of their efforts.

KEY STRATEGIES TO FOSTER TEAM MEMBER SUPPORT PARTNERSHIPS

Inner Loop Key 1: Goal Clarity

When team members understand their mission and goals, the team will work at a higher potential for successful outcomes. The accepted goals must be workable, and all team members should agree upon the steps taken to achieve the goals. Knowing where your team's venture fits in the educational organization strategic plans for quality improvement will guide your team efforts.

While working with the teams in school districts, common themes were generated regarding the necessary elements for teams to function as empowered groups. These themes establish the components of the inner loop of team support partnerships: goal clarity, initiative and creativity, teamwork, information, data assessment, accountability/evaluation, and shared decision making.

Questions to ask pertaining to team goals are as follows: Is goal clarity an attribute of this team? What problem is the team investigating? Was a team action plan developed and followed? In collecting and analyzing data received from the team interview process, certain recurrent themes were evident.

Theme 1 Goal clarity is an integral part of an effective team. All teams studied were successful in achieving their set goals. The solutions to the team problems were attributed to adhering to clear, concise goals. These successful solutions are listed in the teams' improved processes and products (see table 4.2).

Theme 2 A team action plan needs to be developed and followed. A team action plan is important to make certain that the team's objectives are followed. Action plans may be written as formal charters so that all team members are unified as to the long- and short-term objectives that the team will pursue. Many district teams follow their district's strategic plan items. Goal consensus is a powerful tool in arriving at successful team outcomes.

In all of the district teams that were studied, commitment to team goals is very evident in the improved process and product listing (table 4.3). The goals of these teams were met. Your team's goals can also be met. Start by following the strategies for goal clarity, the first step to a solid foundation for teams in your organization.

Inner Loop Key 1: Strategies for Achieving Goal Clarity

1. Define and agree on the team's mission.
2. Formally write down the team's mission statement and post it for all members to see.
3. List individual steps of the team's action plan to reach its goal.
4. Schedule time limits on manageable workloads.
5. Record team efforts and align successes with team goals.

Inner Loop Key 2: Initiative and Creativity

Individual motivation moves team members to become part of an organization's improvement efforts. Using creative talents offers team members the incentive for sustained teamwork. Inducements and resources are not always available in the quantity and degree that are desired, but adding them on to team members' initiative and creative powers will stimulate team activity and lead the team closer to its goals.

Questions to ascertain a team's initiative and creativity are as follows: How are cross-functional team initiative and creativity encouraged in this organization? Who decides which problem is addressed? Was a team action plan developed and followed?

Following are the common themes that were generated by the study teams regarding initiative and creativity.

Theme 1 In the area of initiative and creativity, all team members developed and followed a team action plan. A team's initiative and creativity grow when team members set their own goals. They also increase when the team develops its own techniques and strategies to be followed. Initiative and creativity develop even more when progressive measures and assessments are delegated to team members.

Theme 2 Team members decided which problems should be addressed. Team consensus is a strong method to bring the team together so that all members are on the same page. Misunderstandings and potential conflicts can be averted with this strategy in place.

During the initial quality training of one district team, a pilot team took the unprecedented initiative of altering the process of elementary school daily scheduling. The cross-functional team consisted of primary (grades K–3) and intermediate (grades 4–5) teachers, special-area teachers, and support staff. The team's effort focused on the district's internal customers (staff and students) and used the Plan-Do-Study-Act cycle (also known as the Shewhart Cycle). Brainstorming, flowcharts, and cause-and-effect diagrams were also used. Even though the schools' principals thought the project had too many barriers, the result of the team's effort was a districtwide daily schedule that provided a set block of time for all elementary teachers to design special events and to plan. For special-area teachers, the new schedule resulted in gains in efficiency and effectiveness. The influence of this team's teaming processes was significant:

- Elementary teachers were empowered to work together in planning for and serving their students.
- Events such as student presentations, parent-teacher conferences, and informal grade-level meetings could be scheduled more easily.
- Communication was improved on several levels, including teacher to teacher, teacher to principal, and teacher to parents and/or community members.

The overall result was an improved master schedule without increasing the number of staff, decreasing services to the students, or extending the school day.

Inner Loop Key 2: Strategies for Encouraging Initiative and Creativity

1. Support organizational team initiative through verbal and written charters.
2. Encourage team initiative and creativity during meetings by discussing creative alternatives to problem solving that are aligned with team goals.
3. Understand the needs and interests of team members by communicating alternate solutions to problems during team meetings.
4. Be willing to subordinate individual team member wants in favor of long-term needs of the team when problem solving.
5. Try out new ideas verbally agreed upon by the team at meetings.

Inner Loop Key 3: Teamwork

Teams work best when there are no separate struggles for power. A synergy results in the pooling of each individual member's education, experience, talents, and support for team goals that will sustain team endeavors over a project's span.

Questions that target teamwork are as follows: How is teamwork, coordination of effort, and collective efficiency demonstrated in cross-functional teams in education? What is the team's greatest achievement (turning point) thus far in the team process?

Table 4.2, which delineates the teams' achieved processes and products, shows the common theme that was generated regarding teamwork. It is as follows.

Theme 1 Teamwork, which consists of coordination of effort and collective efficiency, should be demonstrated as the team's greatest achievement. These achievements are charted under two headings: improved product and improved process.

When team members work together, their greatest achievements are evidenced in improved processes and products. Throughout the team study, team members emphasized the point that the need for all to work well with one another cannot be overestimated. The coordination of effort to bring about team successes was the result of both a conscious decision and effort made by all team members.

Inner Loop Key 3: Strategies for Promoting Teamwork

1. Foster whole-team recognition rather than recognizing specific individual team members at meetings and in memos.
2. Sustain team enthusiasm by summarizing positive outcomes at the beginning and end of each meeting.
3. Agree upon the determination that team members' titles are "left at the door" to enable people of different ranks to interact effectively for the common goals of the team.
4. Offer only constructive criticism during meetings when team members work out their differences.
5. Share team member strengths at meetings and assign roles in the team to complement their strong points.

Inner Loop Key 4: Information

A team's success depends on how well members communicate their actions among themselves and to all members of the educational organization. Effective and efficient systems of communication encourage cooperation and lead to suggestions for improving team processes, especially data collection.

Questions to ask regarding needed team information are as follows: What type of information do the project teams need? How are problems identified? How is the data collected (with check sheets, brainstorming, surveys)?

Theme 1 Cross-functional teams in education should collect needed information through several methods. Business and industry leaders have identified planning, organizing, problem solving, and decision making as the primary processes underlying every task in every project. Successful teams have found that they need to be able to develop ideas, identify critical elements, and use significant data.

In order to plan, organize, solve problems, and make decisions efficiently, successful teams have found that they need a set of tools to clearly focus on their effort and to make sure they are productive.

Brainstorming is a tool that meets team members' needs. It is an effective way to get ideas out in a relatively short span of time. Brainstorming really works because *all* ideas are good ideas! In using this technique, you must remember (as in the plus/delta strategy in chapter 2) not to evaluate or criticize team members' ideas. Brainstorming is a great way to encourage team members to participate. With this technique, synergy is created while fostering a sense of teamwork.

Seven Steps for Brainstorming

1. Identify the topic.
2. Present brainstorming questions.
3. Have everyone join in.
4. State ideas or add to someone else's ideas.
5. Record the ideas.
6. Don't criticize or evaluate opinions.
7. Discuss ideas after the brainstorming session is finished.

Remember: *All* ideas are good ideas.

Surveys are extremely effective tools to use from the outset of a team's work, during teaming processes, as well as at the end of a project (see chapter 5, figures 5.1 and 5.2 and table 5.1).

Inner Loop Key 4: Strategies for Sharing Information

1. Make notes on a calendar as to what information is needed and when it is needed.
2. Restate new information at meetings to check for understanding and the need for additional information.
3. Ask for an explanation of words or terms that team members don't understand.
4. Support information avenues by sharing ideas with examples and data in diagrams or charts.
5. Collect data for analysis:
   a. To investigate possible causes (fishbone diagram)
   b. To develop a focus (Pareto chart)
   c. To pinpoint problems with a product or process (run chart)

A fishbone diagram (also called a cause-and-effect or Ishikawa diagram; see figure 6.2) helps you explore, identify, and display the possi-

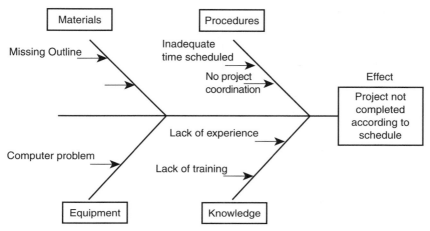

Figure 6.2 *Fishbone diagram.*

ble causes of a problem being studied. The focus should be on the cure of the cause and not on the symptoms of the problem.

A Pareto chart (see figure 6.3) can be used to identify a problem or a root cause or to monitor success of a project. To focus attention on the most important factors of an issue, the bars are displayed from largest on the left to smallest on the right.

A run chart (see figure 6.4) is a live graph that displays data collected from sequential observations. It shows trends within observation points over a period of time.

Inner Loop Key 5: Data Assessment

After collecting meaningful data and identifying root causes of problems, develop appropriate solutions and design an improvement plan to make the necessary changes. Incorporate a Plan-Do-Study-Act strategy. This strategic action plan will ensure that you plan the actions your team intends to take. This will provide the means to check the effectiveness of any actions taken. You can then make any necessary improvements at every step of the team's endeavor as it progresses.

Questions to pose to team members concerning data assessment methods to be used are as follows: How does this team assess data (e.g., with a Pareto chart, a fishbone diagram, or a run chart)? What

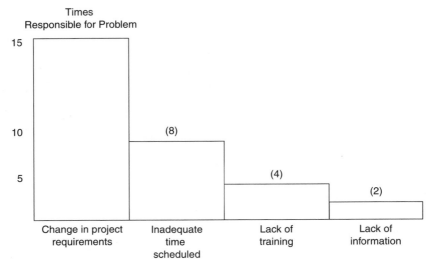

Figure 6.3   *Pareto chart.*

method will the team employ to analyze collected data? What are the steps involved in the data assessment?

Theme 1 Plan the change. Ask questions. Whom will the change impact and how? What changes should be made and in what order should they be made? Where should the team begin? What is the sequence of steps to be taken? When will the team know when the change is complete? How does the team know whether the change is appropriate and adequate?

Theme 2 Do the change. Small-scale implementation of any change is more manageable, and feedback will be available sooner.

Theme 3 Check the change.

- Monitor and adjust
- Gather more data, if necessary.
- Make an educated decision as to how to progress.

Theme 4 Act on the change.

- Make obvious changes in a timely fashion.
- Plan methods to address longer-term issues.
- Follow up on client needs and concerns.

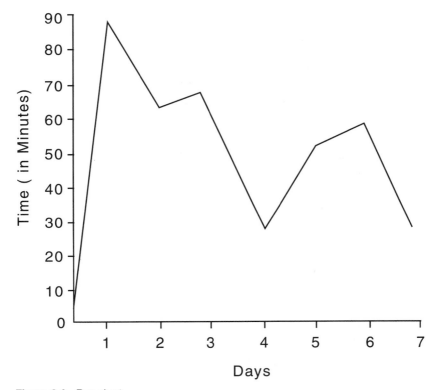

Figure 6.4 *Run chart.*

Does this strategy look and sound familiar? Figure 1.1 (see chapter 1), the Plan-Do-Study-Act cycle, outlines this process for a system or process improvement.

Inner Loop Key 5: Strategies for Supporting Data Assessment

1. Collect meaningful data to pinpoint common sources of inaccurate data and indicate how they can be combated.
2. Include the following in every data document:
   a. Date of collection
   b. Time span covered

  c. Location of data collection

  d. Instruments/methods used

3. Match data collected that addresses the needed change in process or product to help initiate change.

4. Use collected data to do the following:

  a. Understand the current actual situation

  b. Regulate and modify the process

  c. Accept or reject a product or process

5. Incorporate a Plan-Do-Study-Act strategy to check the effectiveness of problem solving:

  a. Plan: Document a needed change aimed at an improvement in the school environment or process.

  b. Do: Carry out the change supported by the data.

  c. Study: Observe or monitor the effects of the change.

  d. Act: Adopt the change or abandon it if the results are not useful.

Inner Loop Key 6: Accountability/Evaluation

Accountability within the team clarifies both who does what and how members work together. Focus should be on how the team will work together. Concerning team accountability/evaluation, make these inquiries: Who is responsible for what on the team? How will the team make decisions? How will the team support these decisions?

Theme 1 Establishing team accountability works best when the members' expertise and experience help to improve operational issues. With the right people on a team, everything eventually falls into place. Having a goal plan is necessary in establishing team accountability. Eventually, team goals should be tied to the strategic planning process.

Employ the use of a team facilitator to further team empowerment. A team facilitator's responsibilities include keeping the team focused and moving in the right direction. Under the facilitator's guidance, team members should review and evaluate team actions and decisions. Effective discussions are necessary for effective meetings, which, in turn, are necessary for a team's outcomes to be effective, efficient, and timely.

Ground rules need to be set for teams. Individual team members' roles on the team should be clarified. With the help of a team facilitator, teams categorize and clarify tasks and activities to be accomplished. High-priority tasks and those that could be delegated or delayed should also be determined to ensure that targeted successful team outcomes occur in a timely manner.

In one middle school team from the research study, volunteers from all organizational levels were asked to be a part of the cross-functional school team that would pursue the National Blue Ribbon Recognition program award. The purpose of the program is to recognize public and private schools for their effectiveness in meeting local, state, and national education goals. Team members included a teacher representative from each department, special-area teachers (technical education, art, home economics, physical education, and music), a counselor, a student council adviser, students, and parents. The team facilitator asked for a volunteer team leader to collect and present the data. A year-long team effort ensued with complete staff involvement.

The team's main task was to gather data and document various teams' efforts in the areas of leadership, teaching environment, curriculum and instruction, student environment, parent and community support, indicators of success, organizational vitality. Also, this cross-functional team was responsible for identifying and acknowledging all contributions that helped their middle school become an exemplary school.

Techniques used by the team included flowcharts in the form of scoreboards and check sheets for data collection and analysis. The middle school was declared a Blue Ribbon School and received national recognition in Washington, D.C.

After being recognized as a school of excellence, staff members in their pursuit of continuous progress and commitment to quality formed teams to create a twelve-month staff calendar. The calendar was used to ensure more effective and efficient scheduling. Also, they created a substitute teacher folder to be used in a teacher's absence to ensure continuous service to students.

Inner Loop Key 6: Strategies for Encouraging Accountability/Evaluation

1. Choose a team leader to guide and manage the activities of the team, which include the following:
   a. Communicate to team members long-range plans, short-term objectives, time schedules, and workable workloads.

    b. Communicate team's progress needs (priorities, workloads, and resources) to the leadership team and the rest of the organization.

    c. Document project by keeping records of meetings and presentations, minutes, agendas, and data related to the project (charts, graphs, etc.).

    d. Remove barriers to team progress by helping to resolve conflicts and by seeking assistance or resources that will enable team members to do the work.

2. Select a team facilitator with people skills, technical skills, and training skills.

3. Choose a team facilitator to help the team focus on its processes rather than its outcomes.

    a. Provide training as needed in the following areas:
- Interpersonal skills (group dynamics)
- Technical skills (problem-solving principles and quality tools)

    b. Help the team deal with conflict by coaching the team leader or team members.

4. Focus upon team members that think less about personal goals and more about the success of the team as a whole.

5. Look for team members that value different ideas and make realistic commitments and then keep them.

Inner Loop Key 7: Shared Decision Making

A team's decision-making process speaks volumes. Well-defined decision-making procedures will ultimately make or break the team. Deciding important issues by consensus supported by the use of data should be encouraged and maintained.

Questions to ask about shared decision making are as follows: What decision-making and problem-solving techniques does this team employ? What are the team's challenges? How are team challenges surmounted?

Theme 1 Decision-making and problem-solving techniques of teams in education should be determined in relationship to the challenges of the problem to be studied. Team challenges usually center around ways to improve a process or finding a root cause of a certain problem in the school district.

Theme 2 Team challenges can be surmounted through dialogue and consensus. Three techniques to use in surmounting the teams' challenges are dialogue/consensus, data collection/analysis, and the use of tools of quality.

Inner Loop Key 7: Strategies for Encouraging Shared Decision Making

1. Suggest discussion methods such as round-robins or brainstorming in order to include all team members.
2. Check the team's understanding of team issues by stating verbally what is and is not agreed upon.
3. Keep comments focused on the topic of discussion and point out relationships between fact and opinions.
4. Avoid judgmental language in team meetings. Remain objective by restating the team's goals.
5. Ask team members for more details (concise examples) or clarification of their ideas (illustrations) before making a judgment.

KEY STRATEGIES TO FOSTER INTERNAL DISTRICT SUPPORT PARTNERSHIPS

Team members need to support each other. District leaders need to support those partnerships with the necessary resources. Themes that establish the middle loop of internal district support partnerships are respect and trust, team training, time resources, recognition, organizational systems, and organizational structures.

Middle Loop Key 1: Respect and Trust

Respect and trust are the cornerstones of educational innovation in schools. Leaders in education need to go beyond *you* ("you do this and that"), or dependence, to *I* ("I can do it"), which is independence, and eventually to *we* ("we will improve our educational system"), or interdependence.

Questions to ask regarding respect and trust are as follows: Are cross-functional teams respected and trusted in this organization? Do the team leader and team administrator model risk taking for teams? Is a safety net provided for risk taking (e.g., "failure is acceptable," "we learn from our mistakes")? Do the team leader and team administrator value the teaming processes?

Theme 1   A supportive and risk-taking environment needs to be created by both the team leaders and team administrator to foster respect and trust in cross-functional teams in education. A good attitude for team members to have when starting a team project is that "everything is a risk, but if something doesn't work out the first time, we'll try again."

The team leader should be a direct, yet tactful, facilitator. Sometimes team leaders must put themselves on the line time and time again for the best interests of the team.

A "never say no" attitude is always helpful to have when working on a team; if one thing doesn't work out, encourage teams to try something else. Keep in mind that there is no one right answer to a problem. Take the time at team meetings to discuss all possibilities and aspects of a problem.

Theme 2   Team members' opinions should be valued to promote respect and trust in teams. Be a strong role model as a team leader: Value team members' opinions. Support communication among team members. Be willing to try new ideas. Encourage the team to take risks.

Be supportive of all team efforts in both word and action. You alone, as a team leader, have the power to create an environment of respect and trust. It must come from you first. Respect and trust will only take hold in an environment that desires and nurtures them.

Openness to Opinions

Both the team administrators and team leader must be open to opinions; such an attitude is a necessary element for a successful team. Keep in mind the following axiom: Educational leaders must give up power to get power.

In the team process, the answers should come from the group process itself and not the district leadership. In order to be really effective, team leaders must possess an openness to the views and positions of others. Team members' opinions and comments must be listened to and respected—team success depends on this fact.

Theme 3 Team encouragement is another important element in establishing respect and trust among teams in education. Having top-down interest in the teaming process is the most powerful way to make changes in a school district. Educational leaders must be very support-ive of teamwork. In some educational organizations, even the hiring process is team-based. Discussing team values in a hiring interview is a great screening tool to assure that future staff members share the belief that teams can influence and guide an organization's improve-ment efforts. A total team support effort in your district is the regener-ating powerhouse that will keep teaming processes alive and well.

Theme 4 Openness to new ideas is an important step toward achiev-ing respect and trust. Openness to new ideas, a respect and trust ele-ment of effective and empowered teams, encourages other possibilities to problem solving to be suggested. Keeping the lines of communica-tion open on the team helps maintain the team's focus on continuously improving team processes.

Middle Loop Key 1: Strategies for Achieving Respect and Trust

1. Encourage team members with direct eye contact and friendly responses to their contributions.
2. Share thoughts and feelings with the team and encourage and support team members' expression of opinions, beliefs, and con-cerns.
3. Move team toward harmony and compromise while using appro-priate humor to reduce tension in the team.
4. Give compliments freely to show team members regard and con-cern.
5. Show confidence in team members' abilities or intentions by entrusting responsibilities to them and supporting their efforts.

Middle Loop Key 2: Team Training

Team-building skills are needed to develop the necessary climate and culture that values shared decision making in teams. Team training also is the vehicle that gives leaders regular and convenient times to generate and develop strategies for the empowerment of their teaming processes in order to carry on the team's continuous improvement efforts.

Team-training questions to consider are as follows: What resources are needed for teams in education to be successful? How much training in team building do the teams in this district possess (e.g., training in problem solving, group dynamics, tools of quality)? Is there a team sponsor (partnership)? Is there a partnership between teams and union leaders in this district?

Theme 1 Resources that include different types of team training are needed for teams in education. The average staff development training time that a district sets aside specifically for teaming processes is usually two and one-half days. In these organizations, team training is considered essential to effective teaming processes. Up-front training—just-in-time training—should be the priority, not "just-in-case" training.

Team training is divided into two parts: interpersonal skills (e.g., conflict resolution, group dynamics) and technical skills (e.g., tools of quality, problem solving). Some districts satisfy the team-training prerequisites by including staff or community members with extensive prior team training in current district teams. Team members with this background are an alternative to hiring outside consultant team trainers. Here is a good analogy: "You get two for the price of one."

Theme 2 Partnership with union leaders is important to team initiatives in educational organizations. Union leaders possessing positive attitudes about the teaming process are bolsters for your district's team initiatives.

When union leaders, with the support of their membership, participate in the teaming process, your district will be more strongly rooted. Union partnership, in the districts in which teams are an integral part of the problem solving and shared decision making, is most supportive.

Theme 3 A team sponsor partnership is helpful in providing resources. A team sponsor partnership between a business organization and an educational one can benefit both. A business partner can offer guidance to district teams for technical skills use (tools of quality, data analysis) in addition to bringing fresh ideas to the educational environment. Business partners also share a different perspective with educational leaders. They bring with them many resources, one of which is monetary support. Educational leaders (e.g., psychologists, guidance counselors, teachers), on the other hand, bring many interpersonal skills (knowledge of conflict resolution, group dynamics, and problem solving) to a business and industry environment.

Middle Loop Key 2: Strategies for Promoting Team Training

1. Develop a network of individuals trained to provide technical and interpersonal skills assistance to teams through verbal and written communications.
2. Provide selected team members with training in technical and interpersonal relationship skills through district staff development workshops, outside consultants, or partnerships with local businesses and experienced community members who possess the needed skills.
3. Use an organizational development specialist or technical adviser to coach school leaders and team members on how to lead and guide team efforts in the district.
4. Educate and train all staff members to realize how their work is influenced by those who preceded them and how their work influences those who follow them.
5. Give access to and support data-based approaches, project planning, management techniques, and group dynamic skills in carefully selected, manageable school improvement projects.

Middle Loop Key 3: Resources/Time

Time for teaming, built into the regular day as it is in business, is necessary for team empowerment in education. For teams to be implemented, developed, and maintained—not just as a beginning movement but as a long-term strategy and the vehicle with which to ensure process and product improvement—weaving ample time into the fabric of the school day, week, and year must be the focus of innovative school leaders. Empowered teams in education will not be realized without including the teaming process in the regularly scheduled school day or week.

The question that should be emphasized concerning the necessary resource of time for teaming process is as follows: When are team meetings scheduled?

Theme 1 Time for teaming processes is a necessary element for effective teams in education. Generally, there isn't enough time during the regularly scheduled school day for team processes to be successful. In many districts, team meetings are held after school hours with some scheduled evening meetings.

One school leader scheduled team meetings in the morning before school started. A little perk for the team members was that the principal paid for the breakfasts. In some districts, after-school meetings were held along with some lunchtime meetings. Only some school districts gave their staff release time and had substitutes take over staff member duties.

A few dedicated team members will contribute their personal time to team initiatives over and over again, but how long will they do that? In one school district, teams received monetary compensation (an established flat hourly rate) for attending team meetings before and after regularly scheduled school hours. This is a nice payoff, but it does not compensate for the lack of sufficient scheduled time necessary for teaming processes to be most effective.

The fact remains that all team members on all district teams studied ranked time for teams as the most important element with which to secure the success of sustained team efforts in education.

Middle Loop Key 3: Strategies for Incorporating Time

1. Study school schedule and then focus on time slot to build in team meetings into the regular school day.
2. Build periodic team meeting into the district's yearly in-service schedule.
3. Work at a comfortable pace but plan well enough in advance so there will be adequate time to prepare for any activity.
4. Pay attention to real constraints to the teaming process (e.g., cur-

riculum requirements, state-mandated staffing issues) to help the team avoid wasted time and naïve solutions.

5. Provide team members release time with substitute coverage to support teaming processes if team time is not built into the schedule.

Middle Loop Key 4: Recognition

The synergy that comes from team members working together productively on an improvement project is usually enough to sustain their enthusiasm and support them through difficult times and hectic schedules in the short term. To sustain empowered teaming processes, educational organizational changes must reflect shared power, shared responsibilities, and, most of all, shared rewards.

Questions to ask concerning recognition of team members include the following: What types of recognition are team members given for their efforts and contributions in education? Are team members recognized? How? Are they rewarded? In what ways?

Theme 1 Recognition of team efforts helps affirm and sustain teaming processes. There are no set policies as to how teams are recognized in many educational organizations. Some small tokens are usually given. Some teams get release time after successful completion of their project. A written certificate of thanks is a common way to recognize team members in education. One district had the honor of receiving an award for team recognition from their city's Council on Excellence. The following year another district team received the Award for Excellence. Plaques were awarded at a chamber of commerce banquet. Press releases with pictures of recipients were published in district newsletters and in the local newspapers.

In one school district, a formal staff recognition program was formed to recognize individual staff members, not teams. Staff members are nominated by their peers. In this district, twelve to eighteen recipients are honored annually. Is this not a sure way to undermine the team process in this organization? If teams are to work, all systems and structures must consistently support teaming efforts.

Middle Loop Key 4: Strategies for Implementing Recognition

1. Affirm team efforts with verbal or written commendations. Such affirmations have a cumulative effect to bolster emotional support.
2. Encourage teamwork through press releases affirming team efforts at organizational meetings.
3. Plan several major districtwide events to recognize the work of teams in the school district, and have team members participate in planning the events.
4. Celebrate team efforts/successes with food and drink to provide a caring team support system in leisure time.
5. Recognize and reward team contributions in ways that are meaningful to team members (ask them for feedback). This creates synergistic cooperation and team spirit.

Middle Loop Key 5: Systems, or How the Organization's Work Gets Done

Systems, groups of related processes, involve thousands of interrelated processes. Processes that make up the educational organization should be studied one at a time (e.g., examine the processes of teaching students, conferencing with parents, assessing learners). Systems in education must be designed to support the goals of the organization. Looking good never replaces doing well.

Middle Loop Key 5: Strategies for Assessing Organizational Systems

1. Begin team training with the school board, superintendents, administrative teams, and the instructional staff.
2. Pursue a joint effort between the school district, the state department of education, and/or a major corporation to participate in team-building activities.
3. Rely on outside consultants whose goal is to empower the district to train itself in team skills.

4. Develop your district's internal systems of coaching supportive groups that will further team building.

Middle Loop Key 6: Structures, or How the Organization Is Constructed

Structures, arrangement of elements and parts of the organization, should foster continuous improvement efforts. Everyone and every part of the educational organization should work to accomplish change for the better. The need for continuous improvement in education is so encompassing and pervasive, everyone in every part of the organization should work toward that priority. Team building is not alchemy. Staff development is necessary, and time must be built into the school schedule for teaming processes.

Ask yourself the following questions: What educational organizational systems and structures support teams in this district? What is my role as a member of the team? Was I selected as a team member based on my hierarchical position (as administrator, supervisor, or teacher) or because of my closeness to the problem? Are team members representative of essential groups?

Organizational systems and structures that support teams in education are apparent in team member and representative group member selection. The largest group of representative members on a team is usually homeroom teachers, followed by special-area teachers, and the smallest group representation consists of students, union officers, and support staff.

Questions to ask when focusing on educational organizational systems and structures are as follows: How are team members selected? What is the member makeup of the district's teams?

Theme 1 Choose team members based on their closeness to problem. Consider the fact that the people at the level at which the work gets done best know where the problems lie. Remember that everyone has a vital role on the team. Team members must figure out what their goals should be, what kinds of problems they should be looking for, where to look for them, and which solutions are important.

Most individuals are selected for teams based on their hierarchical position in the district and closeness to the problem. Team members from the research study noted the importance of members' being close to the problem in order to help arrive at the best workable solution.

Theme 2 Team members are selected in various ways. Some team members volunteer to be on project teams. Some individuals are asked directly by the team administrator or leader to join the team. Use the methods that work best for you in a particular situation.

Theme 3 Representation of essential groups on teams to voice their own concerns is vital to successful outcomes. The persons directly affected by a team's problem-solving and shared decision-making outcomes should be considered first as representative team members. Team administrators and leaders must make every effort and take every step necessary to solicit the many voices of those most affected by the team's decisions. Allow these representatives to define their own versions of quality rather than permitting others who hold more power to speak for them.

Middle Loop Key 6: Strategies for Improving Organizational Structures

1. Hire educational leaders at every level in the district; mentor and model the principles of the district's mission statement.
2. Create conditions that support the district's shared vision and principles by recruiting and selecting team members by carefully matching potential members' abilities, aptitudes, and interests with the team's mission.
3. Identify all stakeholders that share equal responsibility for providing the best learning environment for children to grow, and include them on specific teams.
4. Include educational leaders, school board members, business leaders, principals, teachers, parents, students, and community members on teams to voice their vested interests in the learning environment.

KEY STRATEGIES TO DEVELOP EXTERNAL CLIENT SUPPORT PARTNERSHIPS

Outer Loop Key 1: Family

Besides students, parents benefit most immediately from the strength of a quality educational system. Only they can tell you what they want for their children and how they want it. Educators must work with parent input to determine their needs and collaborate with them in providing quality outcomes and services within professional educational parameters.

Outer Loop Key 2: Community

A major goal of quality teams in education is selecting learning outcomes that are based on the needs and wants of the community. The diverse skills, resources, and support offered by community members help teams make informed choices.

Outer Loop Key 3: Agencies

Local, state, and governmental agencies act as advocates of quality education by supplying assisted technology to augment the curriculum and the work of teams. Identifying and developing resource people within the educational system are initial priorities. It is almost always necessary to recruit technical resources from the outside as well. These resource persons are experts in their fields and will often coach teams in how to lead and will guide their efforts under study.

Outer Loop Key 4: Business and Industry

In addition to the obvious financial support that a business partnership brings to education, there are some not so obvious perks that business/industry can share with education, if only asked to do so. Business/industry personnel can share assistance in extra training in project management, group process, statistics, and tools of quality. Business partners can often act in the capacity of project team consultants or quality advisers in addition to contributing needed monetary support.

Considering External Clients

Identifying external client needs and concerns is crucial to establishing empowerment of teams in education. This strategy is especially effective in school districts that have not established close contact with their external clients.

When including external clients on teams, it is necessary to meet and talk to each other as customers and suppliers. Discuss issues such as what they need and what the school district needs to establish in the partnership. The external clients of a school district should be its best public relations agents. The district's goal should be not only to meet the clients' expectations but to exceed them. The communication loop, discussed in the following section, is the ways and means to help accomplish this goal.

Strategies for Building External Client Support Partnerships

Step 1: Make a list of external clients. Include the following:
- Families of students in the district
- Community members
- Local, state, and governmental agencies
- Businesses and industries

Step 2: Call external clients at home or business. Keep records of the calls as follows:
- No answer: Note that there was no contact and to try again
- Busy signal: Call again
- Answering machine: Leave message
- Phone answered: Go to step 3

Step 3: Ask external clients to participate in team activities. Note their responses:
- Answer no: Ask/record client's needs and concerns at this time
- Answer yes: Go to step 4

Step 4: Notify external clients of a district informational meeting about teaming or invite clients to the first team meeting.
- Follow up with formal written invitation.

Step 5: Survey clients by mail asking them what their needs and concerns are and informing them of the district's needs and concerns in establishing external client support partnerships.

Step 6: Visit external clients to discuss issues of their and the district's needs and concerns.

Step 7: Make a modified list of external clients for future team endeavors.

Step 8: Send letters to external clients on the modified list to ask for their team participation at another time. Be clear about school district expectations.

THE COMMUNICATION LOOP

The team empowerment model for education incorporates the following three cornerstones:

- Team support partnerships
- Internal district support partnerships
- External client support partnerships

The communication loop supports these necessary partnerships. Without this strategy, team achievements will not be realized.

By developing and managing flexible yet controlled support partnerships, continuous educational improvements can be monitored. A team's success depends not only on how well team members communicate with each other but how well they share their improvement efforts with the various levels of the organization. This type of communication encourages cooperation from colleagues and often leads to suggestions for improving team processes. Teams, to establish effective communication patterns, must establish a manner and format of sharing the team's progress among team members and others who are likely to be affected by or interested in its activities. Team empowerment is increased when effective and efficient methods of disseminating team updates are tailored to organizational members' needs and wants. An option would be to poll both internal and external clients as to which methods of information dispersal would best suit both individual and district needs. Solicit answers to the following questions: Which forms of communication do cross-functional teams employ in this organization? Which communication methods are used to inform members of team meetings, team agenda, and team progress? After each meeting, is feedback provided to the staff?

Theme 1 The communication methods employed by cross-functional teams in education are varied among successful teams. Written memos prove to be a most effective means of communication among team members and district staff. Memos with minutes from the last team meeting and an agenda for the next meeting are sent to all members. Setting the time, place, and agenda for the next team meeting during a meeting is helpful.

In some districts, team updates are shared at faculty meetings every month. Sending memos to all staff members after each team meeting is a practice in some schools. One very innovative and energetic team leader sends out a newsletter after each time her team meets. She includes such items as "how things are going" and "do you have any suggestions?" This truly has been an extremely powerful communication tool in her district.

Another method of team communication is posting team memos and/or minutes in the faculty lounge for all staff to see. Some teams even post fishbone diagrams and Pareto charts to emphasize team results.

Strategies for Achieving Successful Communication

1. Seek information on and opinions of team members, organizational staff, and both internal and external clients as to their preferred communication methods with which to disseminate team efforts.
2. Conduct open discussions encouraging parent and community feedback as to how your educational system is doing and whether your services meet their needs. Ask specific questions (e.g., "What are three things we can do to improve the quality of our district's educational services?").
3. Acknowledge the need for feedback and understand the context of the feedback by reviewing the actions and decisions that led up to the moment.
4. Notify principals, supervisors, and other vested clients in advance and tell them exactly why, how, and when data will be collected.
5. Explain to organizational staff members that the goal of data collection is to identify how systems operate and not to blame individuals for problems within them.

The district's internal clients (students, teachers) and external clients (community, local agencies) should boast about how much they benefit from what you do for them. To attain this goal, reliable communication strategies must be in place to gather the information about what they need and want. The ultimate goal should be to exceed your clients' needs, not merely meet them. Effective communication strategies will make this a reality in your organization. Give them a test run. You have nothing to lose and a lot to gain.

REALITY CHECK! CREATE A BALANCE

Your journey to establishing team empowerment is not an easy one. You are striving for that perfect balance among the three partnerships: team member support, internal district support, and external client support. Your progress is dependent on people and resources, and it requires time to implement, integrate, and refine. Essentially, team empowerment is all about leadership. It is about how you, as an educational leader, realize a vision of the future by making that vision manageable. A manageable vision must be based on what your clients want, but most of all on what the educational organization is capable of delivering. You must be confident in your own abilities and you must not compromise on personal and professional ethics in guiding your educational organization improvement efforts through team building. A truly effective vision is inspired on two levels: the welfare of both internal and external clients and the infinite creative capacity of all of the individuals who make up the educational organization. A visionary leader never loses sight of either.

Together these interrelated groups form the partnerships to unlock the door to team empowerment in education. Under your leadership, team members—confident with securing needed resources, technical and interpersonal skills supported by educational systems and structures, and strengthened by external client support—will provide the security system to sustain true team empowerment in your organization over a long period of time.

Balanced partnerships facilitate empowered teams. Teams that are balanced and proportional in design, that include all clients related to the problem being studied, are crucial. Having a team with a balanced participation of members is necessary for optimum problem solving, shared decision making, and application of solutions. Including needed representative members on a team is necessary for all internal and external clients to voice their own concerns. This desired balanced participation will establish the equality of amount, force, effect, and influence needed to arrive at the best possible solution to any problem. Harmonious intent and direction and completion of a project results from planned and orderly member selection. Arrangement of all key players ensures continuous improvements at all organization levels. It is in your power. Remember, team empowerment is all about your leadership beliefs and practices—you must give up a little power to gain more power.

Finding the right mix to improve team performance during process improvement tasks is important in establishing team success. A structured approach to problem solving, decision making, and process improvement leads to more balanced participation among team members. More balanced participation, however, does not alone influence team performance. Social elements, such as the level of conversation in the group during an unstructured task and whether a team member contributes ideas at a higher level than others, has a larger influence on team performance. As a result, selection of members should be considered an important means of influencing team interaction and performance. Careful selection can ensure that there are members on the team who are able and willing to contribute and that those individuals with high skills in process management are present. Training, through team building or other exercises, becomes the alternative method of ensuring the team has these characteristics.

A paradigm shift is slowly occurring in education today to reflect the wisdom of an old African proverb: "It takes a village to raise a single child." The essence of this saying is reflected in the growing number of educators adopting a systems perspective and employing shared decision making in teams at all levels of the organization.

This new shift in thought and action encourages the collaborative efforts of teachers, students, parents, community members, school board members, and education, business, and industry leaders to work together to foster quality in education. Effective strategies extending beyond the current boundaries of traditional education are necessary to provide the level of educational experiences and skills that will be required in the future. You must be open-minded about educational redesign through your teaming processes. Employing the team empowerment model for education (figure 6.1) requires that ideas not be constrained by the limitations of what can easily be done within your current systems and structures. Explore new possibilities together with your partners for designing the future of education in your organization. Through the power of teams, greater educational effectiveness and efficiency will ensure the promise of tomorrow for students and all other clients of education. You may very well be the change agent that your district and all of education have been waiting for. In addition to the rewards that team successes bring to your school or district, you and your teams can possibly alter the course of education for the future.

Teams in education are a new concept. Implementing them is not an arbitrary process and should be orchestrated by a committed and open leadership that supports partnerships with all the clients of education. The results will be to produce students and staff with expanding abilities, interests, character, growth, and self-confidence. As the spirit of teaming processes becomes an integral part of your educational system, all clients of education will together foster quality efforts—no barriers, no factions, all one team working to create a new and improved system of education. Therein lies the ultimate power of teams in education.

FIND YOUR OWN FORMULA

Employing teaming in your organization is a new, smarter way to manage and improve the education process. The use of teams is a method that works better in today's rapidly changing and very competitive world. The old approach to delivering and managing educational services needs to change to ensure quality educational leadership that will take our schools into the next millennium.

This new quality leadership ranks client focus as the number one priority. Recognizing that all work in a school district is a process is a close second. Curriculum development, instruction, and assessment are not an arbitrary series of actions. The systems and structures of a school district can and must be studied, measured, analyzed, and improved. Unity of purpose coupled with a clear and understood vision of continuous improvement is another principle of quality leadership.

This type of environment encourages total commitment from staff members and fosters teamwork and partnerships with everyone in the educational system. This environment is manifest in the common goals of all educators on behalf of learners and the community. This relationship also extends to the suppliers of curriculum and other materials, local community groups, and regulatory agencies, recognizing them as interdependent parts of the entire educational system.

The rest of the current school year will go by whether you are doing something to introduce or improve teaming processes in your school district or not. If you made it this far in this book, you are serious about having effective decision-making and problem-solving teams in your district. Put *teaming strategies* on a project status mode in your district and you will have them.

If you don't have a plan, you will be a stepping-stone for those who do. If you have a clear-cut strategy and the courage, commitment, and energy to execute that strategy at a project level, you can have successful teams working toward continuous improvement in your district. The key to managing this is having and implementing the consciously designed strategies in this book. This may be your chance to change education for the better; it's time to begin.

If you have been doing your homework, you have already acquired some essential knowledge and tools needed to work toward successful teaming processes. You've identified the basic team considerations, dimensions, existing team efforts, and the strategies to use to ensure team empowerment. You've also identified the payoffs of using teaming processes. Whatever your circumstances, giving teams a chance will bring out improved conditions in your organization.

You are now equipped to give teams a chance to bring about improvement one step, one goal, and one priority at a time. Using the tools you have acquired, you can focus on your organization's top priority and design a knowledge- and results-based strategy for change. Apply the team empowerment model for education and take the definitive actions needed to experience successful teaming processes in your educational organization.

Good luck to you!

Glossary

Definitions have been derived from a review of team-related literature.

cause-and-effect diagram An illustration outline representing the relation-ship between some effect and all the possible causes. A well-detailed dia-gram will take on the shape of fish bones; it is sometimes called a fishbone diagram.

client Can be internal or external. Internal clients are the recipients within an organization of its output, that is, its products and/or services. External cli-ents, who are not part of the organization, are also recipients of its products, information, and/or services (Scholtes, 1994).

continuous improvement Ongoing improvement of process or products through incremental change and breakthrough improvements (Bradley, 1993).

cooperative-learning team A group consisting of students working together rather than alone. Class members are involved in decision making about curriculum content in their classroom, classroom rules, and consequences.

cross-functional team A group consisting of members of different depart-ments in an organization; persons with different roles who come together for problem solving and shared decision making relative to larger organiza-tional issues to improve organizational processes (Wellins, Byham, & Wil-son, 1991).

empowerment A deeply personal process of recognizing meaning, which is made within particular historical, cultural, and economic contexts. Enabling one to recognize, create, and channel one's own power by giving that per-son the authority to make decisions.

flowchart A step-by-step procedure diagram used to plan stages of a project or to describe a process that is to be studied.

Pareto chart A special form of vertical bar graph that helps determine which problems to solve and in what order.

Plan-Do-Study-Act (PDSA) cycle A four-step quality improvement process: (1) develop a plan for improvement; (2) carry out the plan; (3) observe the results; (4) study the results to determine what was learned and what can be predicted (Deming, 1986).

problem solving A systematic method of identifying key problems and finding and implementing solutions.

process patterns A systematic series of actions, for example, use of data techniques, team goal setting, and tracking of teams directed toward problem solving and shared decision making.

quality Meeting and exceeding the client's needs and expectations and then continuing to improve; conformance to the client's requirements by defining what the client wants, describing it, and then meeting those requirements exactly (Deming, 1986).

restructuring The second wave of school reform that includes the development of a collegial environment with shared decision making among students and staff. Emphasis is on higher-order thinking skills.

run chart A live graph that displays data from sequential observations of a process.

shared decision making Participation and leadership distributed among members of an organization. Involvement in important decisions affecting students, classrooms, and schools in an educational environment (Piore and Sabel, 1984).

systems improvement Ongoing improvement of processes or products through incremental change or breakthrough improvements.

team building Activities to create understanding in a team to help members work together in unison (Scholtes, 1994).

teaming "Activity in which team members . . . seek knowledge that will serve action . . . both to promote learning . . . and to contribute to general knowledge" (Argyris, Putnum, & Smith, 1990).

tools of quality Data-based instruments (e.g., Pareto chart, cause-and-effect diagram, run chart) used by teams as they address school district issues for improvement.

transformational leadership Value-added leadership that facilitates the redefinition of organizational mission and vision and fosters active staff participation and the restructuring of their systems for goal accomplishment, that is, to generate educational change (Sergiovanni, 1992; Roberts, 1985).

Reference List

Abbot, J. E. (1998). *Quality team learning for schools: A principal's perspective.* Milwaukee, WI: ASQ Quality Press.

Abernethy, P. E., & Serfase, R. W. (1992). One district's quality improvement story. *Educational Leadership, 50*(3), 14.

Adams, W. F., & Bailey, G. D. (1989). Principal leadership behaviors: Making a choice. *NASSP Bulletin, 73*(516), 86–91.

Alavi, M., Keen, P. G. (1989). Business teams in an information age. *The Information Society, 6*(4), 179–195.

Allan, J. (1998). *Sharpen your team skills in time management.* New York: McGraw-Hill.

Argyris, C., Putnum, R., & Smith, D. (1990). *Action science.* San Francisco: Jossey-Bass.

Avolia, B., Waldman, D., & Einstein, W. (1988). Transformational leadership in a management game situation. *Group and Organization Studies, 131*(1), 59–80.

Barth, R. S. (1990). *Improving schools from within.* San Francisco: Jossey-Bass.

Benjamin, S., & Gard, J. (1993). Creating a climate for change: Students, teachers, administrators working together. *NASSP Bulletin, 77*(552), 63–67.

Bentley, T. J. (1998). *Sharpen your team's skills in creativity.* New York: McGraw-Hill.

Berry, J. E., & Stickel, S. A. (1994). *Team building for better decision-making: An interdisciplinary course for educational leaders.* Paper presented at the annual meeting of the Eastern Educational Research Association, Sarasota, FL.

Betts, F. (1992). How systems thinking applies to education. *Educational Leadership, 50*(3), 38–41.

Blackmore, J. (1989). Changing from within: Feminist educators and administrative leadership. *Peabody Journal of Education, 66*(3), 17.

Bolin, F. S. (1989). Empowering leadership. *Teachers College Record*, *91*(1), 81–96.

Bolman, L. G., & Deal, T. E. (1994). Leadership. *Educational Administration Quarterly*, *30*(1), 97–101.

Bonstingl, J. J. (1992a). The quality revolution in education. *Educational Leadership*, *50*(3), 4–9.

Bonstingl, J. J. (1992b). *School of quality: An introduction to total quality management in education*. Alexandria, VA: Association for Supervision and Curriculum Development.

Bonstingl, J. J. (1992c). The total quality classroom. *Educational Leadership*, *49*(6), 66–70.

Bradley, L. H. (1993). *Total quality management for schools*. Lancaster, PA: Technomic Press.

Bragar, J. (1992). The customer-focused quality leader. *Quality Progress*, *25*(5), 53.

Brouillette, L. (1994). *A geology in school reform: Past reforms interact with new as a school district implements shared decision making*. Paper presented at the annual meeting of the American Educational Research Association, New Orleans, LA.

Callahan, R. (1962). *Education and the cult of efficiency*. Chicago: University of Chicago Press.

Capper, C. A., & Jamison, M. T. (1993). Let the buyer beware: Total quality management and educational research and practice. *Educational Researcher*, *22*(8), 15–30.

Caravatta, M. (1997). *Let's work smarter, not harder: How to engage your entire organization in the execution of change*. Milwaukee, WI: ASQ Quality Press.

Carnegie Task Force on Teaching as a Profession. (1986). *A nation prepared: Teachers for the 21st century*. New York: Carnegie Corporation.

Church, E. B. (1997). *Group time*. New York: Scholastic.

Conley, S. C. & Bacharach, S. B. (1990). From school-site management to participatory school-site management. *Phi Delta Kappan*, *71*(7), 539–544.

Csikzentmihalyi, M. (1990). *Flow: The psychology of optimal experience*. New York: Harper Row.

Cuban, L. (1984). *How teachers taught: Constancy and change in American classrooms. 1890–1980*. New York: Longman.

Darling-Hammond, L., & Berry, B. (1988). *The evolution of teacher policy*. Washington, DC: Rand Corporation.

Darling-Hammond, L., Chajet, J., & Robertson, P. (1996). Restructuring schools for high performance. In S. Furhman & J. O'Day (Eds.), *Rewards and reform: Creating educational incentives that work.* San Francisco: Jossey-Bass.

David, J. (1989). Synthesis of research on school-based management. *Educational Leadership, 46*(8), 50–53.

David, J. L. (1991). What it takes to restructure education. *Educational Leadership, 48*(8), 15.

Davis, S. M., & Lawrence, P. R. (1977). *Matrix.* Reading, MA: Addison-Wesley.

Deming, W. E. (1986). *Out of crisis.* Cambridge: Massachusetts Institute of Technology Press.

Deming, W. E. (1989). *A system of profound knowledge.* (1989, July). Paper presented at the meeting of the Institute of Management Sciences, Osaka, Japan.

Dereshiwsky, M. I. (1993). *Assessing learning for leadership: A multimethod qualitative evaluation of the 1992 Arizona leadership academy.* Paper presented at the Pacific Rim Symposium on Higher Education Evaluation, Hilo, HI.

Doyle, D., & Kearns, D. (1988). *Winning the brain race.* Fortuna, CA: ISC Press.

Eichelberger, R. T. (1989). *Disciplined inquiry.* White Plains, NY: Longman Publishing Group.

Erlandson, D. A. & Bifano, S. L. (1987). Teacher empowerment: What the research says to the principal. *NASSP Bulletin, 71*(503), 31–36.

Feeston, K. R. (1992). Getting started with TQM. *Educational Leadership, 50*(30), 10–13.

Fields, J. C. (1994). *Total quality for schools: A guide for implementation.* Milwaukee, WI: ASQC Quality Press.

Fossey, R. (1992). *Site-based management in a collective bargaining environment: Can we mix oil and water?* Paper presented at the Education Law Seminar of the National Organization on Legal Problems of Education, Breckenridge, CO.

Fullan, M. (1991). *The new meaning of educational change.* New York: Teachers College Press.

Fullan, M. (1993). *Change forces.* New York: Falmer Press.

Fullan, M., & Hargreaves, A. (1991). *What's worth fighting for? Working together for your school.* Toronto: Ontario Public School Teachers' Federation.

Fullan, M. & Hargreaves, A. (1996). *What's worth fighting for in your school* (2nd ed.). New York: Teachers College Press.

Gardner, J. W. (1990). *On leadership*. New York: The Free Press.

Gersick, C. J., & Davis-Sacks, M. L. (1990). Summary: Task forces. In J. R. Hackman (Ed.), *Groups that work (and those that don't)* (146–154). San Francisco: Jossey-Bass.

Glasser, W. (1990a). *The quality school*. New York: Harper and Row.

Glasser, W. (1990b). The quality school. What motivates the ants? *Phi Delta Kappan*, *71*(6), 25–35.

Goldman, J. P. (1992). When participatory management attracts no buyers. *School Administrator*, *49*(1), 15.

Gonder, P. O., & Hymes, D. (Eds.). (1994). *Improving school climate and culture*. (AASA Critical Issues Report No. 27). Arlington, VA: American Association of School Administrators.

Green, J. (1987). Transforming teaching through intellectualizing the work of teachers. In J. Smythe (Ed.), *Educating teachers: Changing the nature of pedagogical knowledge* (155–168). London: Falmer Press.

Hacker, M. E. (1999). Team technology. *Quality Progress*, *32*(1), 61–63.

Hackman, J. R. (1990). *Groups that work (and those that don't)*. San Francisco: Jossey-Bass.

Hargreaves, A. (1994). *Changing teachers, changing times: Teachers' work and culture in the postmodern age*. New York: Teachers College Press.

Hargreaves, A., Earl, L., & Ryan, J. (1996). *Schooling for change*. London: Falmer Press.

Harris, M. F., and Harris, R. C. (1992). Glasser comes to a rural school. *Educational Leadership*, *50*(3), 18–21.

Heald-Taylor, G. (1991). *An investigation of the relationship among school goal setting procedures, school goal consensus and the cohesiveness of a school's culture*. Doctoral dissertation, The Ontario Institute for Studies in Education, Toronto.

Hill, S., & Hill, T. (1991). *The collaborative classroom*. NH: Heinemann Educational Books, Inc.

Horine, J. E., Hailey, W., & Rubach, L. (1994). Transforming schools. *Quality Progress*, *26*(10) 31–33.

Johnson, D. W., & Johnson, F. P. (1982). *Joining together group theory and group skills*. Englewood Cliffs, NJ: Prentice Hall.

Johnson, D. W., & Johnson, F. P. (1987). *Joining together* (3rd ed.). Englewood Cliffs, NJ: Prentice Hall.

Klees, E. (1998). *One plus one equals three strengths—Pairing man/woman strengths*. TN: Ingram Book Company.

Kushman, J. W. (1992). The organizational dynamics of teacher workplace commitment: A study of urban elementary and middle schools. *Educational Administration Quarterly, 28,* 5–42.

La Brecque, R. (1998). *Effective department and team leaders—A practical guide.* Washington, DC: C. G. Publishing Company.

Larson, C. E., & LaFasto, M. J. (1989). *Team work.* Newbury Park, CA: Sage Publications.

Lawrence, P. R., & Lorsch, J. W. *Organization and environment.* Burr Ridge, IL: R. D. Irwin/McGraw-Hill.

Leithwood, K., Dart, B., Jantzi, D., & Steinback, R. (1992). *Fostering organizational learning: A study of British Columbia's intermediate developmental site initiatives (final report).* British Columbia: British Columbia Ministry of Education.

Leithwood, K. A. (1992). The move toward transformational leadership. *Educational Leadership, 49*(5), 10.

Lezotte, L. W. (1991). Effective schools the second generation: Feminist educators and administrative leadership. *Peabody Journal of Education, 66*(3), 17.

Lieberman, A. (1988a). Expanding the leadership team. *Educational Leadership, 45*(5), 4–8.

Lieberman, A. (1988b). Teachers and principals: Turf, tension, and new tasks. *Phi Delta Kappan, 69*(9), 649.

Lieberman, A. (1995). *The work of restructuring schools: Building from the ground up.* New York: Teachers College Press.

Lieberman, A. (Ed.). (1989). *Building a professional culture in schools.* New York: Teachers College Press.

Lieberman, A., Darling-Hammond, L., & Zuckerman, D. (1991). *Early lessons in restructuring schools.* New York: National Center for Restructuring Education, Schools and Teaching.

Louis, K., & Miles, M. (1990). *Improving the urban high school.* New York: Teachers College Press.

Louis, K. S., & Smith, B. (1991). Restructuring, teacher engagement and school culture: Perspectives on school reform and the improvement of teachers' work. *School Effectiveness and School Improvement, 2*(91), 34–52.

Maeroff, G. I. (1993). Building teams to rebuild schools. *Phi Delta Kappan, 74*(7), 518–519.

McIntyre, M. G. (1998). *Management team handbook—Five key strategies for maximizing group performance.* San Francisco: Jossey-Bass.

Melvin, C. (1991). Restructuring schools by applying Deming's management theories. *Journal of Staff Development, 12*(3), 16–20.

Melvin, C. A. (1991). Translating Deming's 14 points for education. *The School Administrator, 9*(48), 19–23.

Mitchell, D. E., & Tucker, S. (1992). Leadership as a way of thinking. *Educational Leadership, 49*(5), 30–35.

Moenart, R. K., & Souder, W. E. (1990). An analysis of the use of extra-functional information: review and model. *Journal of Product Innovation Management, 7*(3), 91–107.

Murphy J. (Ed.). (1990). *The educational reform movement of the 1980s: A comprehensive analysis.* Berkeley, CA: McCutchan.

National Governors Association. (1986). *Time for results.* Washington, DC: National Governors Association.

Nelson, W. (1993). TQM in rural education—Managing schools from a business perspective. *Rural Educator, 15*(2), 21–22.

Newmann, F., & Wehlage, G. (1995). *Successful school restructuring.* Alexandria, VA: Association for Supervision and Curriculum Development.

Nutt, P. C. (1986). Tactics of implementation. *Academy of Management Journal, 29,* 230–261.

O'Brien, J. D. (1994). Cross-functional teams build a "big picture" attitude. *Supervisory Management, 39*(10), 1–2.

O'Looney, J. (1993). Redesigning the work of education. *Phi Delta Kappan, 75*(5), 376.

Orsburn, J. D., & Moran, L. (1998). *The new self-directed work teams: Mastering the challenge.* (2nd ed.). New York: McGraw-Hill.

Peters, T. (1988). Restoring American competitiveness: Looking for new models of organizations. *The Academy of Management Executives, 11*(2) 103–108.

Peters, T. J., & Austin, N. J. (1985). *A passion for excellence.* New York: Random House.

Pinto, M. B., Pinto, J. K., & Prescott, J. E. (1993). Antecedents and consequences of project team cross-functional cooperation. *Management Science, 39*(10), 1295.

Piore, M. J., & Sabel, C. F. (1984). *The second industrial divide.* New York: Basic Books.

Posner, B. Z., & Kouzes, J. M. (1987). *Leadership challenge.* San Francisco: Jossey-Bass.

Raelin, J. A. (1989). How to give your teachers autonomy without losing control. *The Executive Educator, 11*(2), 19–20.

Rees, F. (1997). *Teamwork from start to finish: 10 steps to results.* San Francisco: Jossey-Bass.

Research Policy Committee of the Committee for Economic Development. (1985). *Investing in our children.* New York: Committee for Economic Development.

Reukert, R. W., & Walker, O. C. (1987). Marketing's interaction with other functional units: Conceptual framework and empirical evidence. *Journal of Marketing, 51,* 1–19.

Rhodes, L. A. (1990a). The Deming superintendent. Beyond your beliefs: Quantum leaps to quality schools. *The School Administrator, 47*(11), 24–25.

Rhodes, L. A. (1990b). Why quality is within our grasp . . . if we reach. *School Administrator, 41*(10), 31–34.

Rhodes, L. A. (1992). On the road to quality. *Educational Leadership, 49*(6), 76–80.

Rippa, S. A. (1988). *Education in a free society: An American history.* New York: Longman.

Roberts, N. (1985). Transforming leadership: A process of collective action. *Human Relations, 38*(11), 1023–1046.

Sagor, R. (1996). *Local control and accountability: How to get it, keep it, and improve school performance.* Thousand Oaks, CA: Corwin Press.

Salisbury, D. (1992). A special report: Toward a new generation of schools: The Florida school year 2000 initiative. *Educational Technology, 32*(7), 7.

Saronson, S. B. (1990). *The predictable failure of education reform.* San Francisco: Jossey-Bass.

Scholtes, P. R. (1994). *The team handbook for educators.* Madison, WI: Joiner Associates.

Senge, P. M. (1990). *The fifth discipline. The art and practice of the learning organization.* New York: Doubleday.

Sergiovanni, T. J. (1990). *Value-added leadership: How to get extraordinary performance in schools.* San Francisco: Harcourt Brace Jovanovich.

Sergiovanni, T. J. (1992). Why we should seek substitutes for leadership. *Educational Leadership, 49*(5), 41–45.

Shedd, J., & Bacharach, S. (1991). *Tangled hierarchies: Teachers as professionals and the management of schools.* San Francisco: Jossey-Bass.

Simon, R. (1987). Empowerment as a pedagogy of possibility. *Language Arts, 64*(4), 370–382.

Sirotnik, K. A. (1989). The school as the center of change. In J. T. Sergiovanni (Ed.), *Schooling for tomorrow* (89–113). Needham Heights, MA: Allyn & Bacon.

Sizer, T. R. (1984). *Horace's compromise: The dilemma of the American high school.* Boston: Houghton Mifflin.

Smialek, M. A. (1995). Total quality in K–12 education: Meeting educational leadership challenges using the power of teams. *Quality Progress, 28*(5), 69–72.

Smialek, M. A. (1996). *Team process patterns in education K–12: A comparative study.* Pittsburgh, PA: University of Pittsburgh, dissertation.

Smialek, M. A. (1998). Team empowerment: A simple and easy solution. *Quality Progress, 31*(9), 65–71.

Smith, W. E. (1993). *Teacher's perceptions of role change through shared decision making: A two-year case study.* Paper presented at the annual meeting of the American Educational Research Association, Atlanta, GA.

Stampen, J. (1987). Improving the quality of education: W. Edward Deming and effective schools. *Contemporary Education Review, 3*, 432–433.

Stoll, L., & Fink, D. (1996). *Changing our schools.* Philadelphia: Open University Press.

Syer, J., & Connolly, C. (1977). *How teamwork works: The dynamics of effective team development.* New York: McGraw-Hill.

Thomas, K. *Conflict and conflict management: Handbook of industrial and organizational psychology.* Dunnette, MD: Rand-McNally.

U.S. Department of Labor. (1992). *Learning a living: A blueprint for high performance, a SCANS report for America 2000.* Washington, DC: Department of Labor.

Vance, M., & Deacon, D. (1996). *Break out of the box: A new leadership mode for high personal achievement.* Franklin Lakes, NJ: Career Press.

Walton, M. (1990). *Deming management at work.* New York: Putnam.

Weaver, C. N. (1993). How to use process improvement teams. *Quality Progress, 26*(12), 67.

Webb, R. B. & Sherman, R. R. (1989). *Schooling and society* (2nd ed.). New York: Collier Macmillan.

Weiss, C. H. (1993). Shared decision making about what? A comparison of schools with and without teacher participation. *Teachers College Record, 95*(1), 87.

Wellins, R. S., Byham, W. C., & Wilson, J. M. (1991). *Empowered teams.* San Francisco: Jossey-Bass.

Wheatley, M. J. (1992). *Leadership and the new science: Learning about organization from an orderly universe.* San Francisco: Berrett-Koehler.

White, P. A. (1989). An overview of school-based management: What does the research say? *NASSP Bulletin, 73*(518), 1–8.

Wilson, J. M., & George, J. A. (1997). *The team leader's survival guide.* New York: McGraw-Hill.

Wimpelberg, R. K., & Boyd, W. L. (1990). Restructured leadership: Directed autonomy in an age of educational reform. *Planning and Changing, 21*(4), 250.

Wind, Y. (1981). Marketing and the other business functions. In J. N. Sheth (Ed.), *Research in marketing* (237–264). Greenwich, CT: JAI Press.

Wise, A., & Darling-Hammond, L. (1985). Teacher evaluation and teacher professionalism. *Educational Leadership. 42*(4), 28–33.

Wosner, R. L., & Damme, S. R. (1993). A review of Peter Senge's examination of learning organizations: Implications for vocational special needs programs. *Journal for Vocational and Special Needs Education, 15*(3), 53–56.

Zeichner, K. (1991). Contradictions and tensions in the professionalization of teaching and the democratization of schools. *Teachers College Record, 92*(3), 364–365.

Zuckerman, D. W. (1993). *Necessary but insufficient: Three linked efforts to restructure New York City public schools in 1990–1991.* Paper presented at the annual meeting of the American Educational Research Association, Atlanta, GA.

Index

accountability: questions to ask, 74; strategies for, 75–76; theme, 74–76

advantages of teams. *See* teams, advantages and benefits of

agencies, 87

balance, creating a, 16, 19, 91–94

brainstorming, 67–70; seven steps for, 70

business/industry, vi, 87

cause and effect diagram, 71

challenge of an education leader, 3, 45

change: educational, v, vii, 6, 20; transformational, v; resistance to, 45

clients: external, 87–89; internal, 90, 91

collaboration, 17

communication loop, 88, 88–90; questions to ask, 89–90; strategies for, 90–91; theme, 89–90

community, 87

cross-functional teams, 7, 22–24, 26, 33

data assessment: questions to ask, 71–73; strategies for, 73–74; themes, 72–73

dimensions of teams: team advantages, 21–24; team disadvantages, 24–26

education: future of, 46; quality in, 28

empowerment: staff, 13–14; team, 52–59, 61–65, 94

empowerment model for teams. *See* teams, empowerment model for education

environment, supportive and risk-taking, 78–79

evaluation, 71–73

family, 86–87

fishbone diagram, 71, 90

formula, finding your own, 93–94

goal clarity: questions to ask, 63; strategies for, 66; themes, 65–66

group behavior problems, 26

group process: rules for, 18–19; in school, 19–20

improvement: continuous, 4; in
     school, 28
information, 28; questions to ask, 69;
     strategies for, 70–71; theme,
     70–71
initiative and creativity: questions to
     ask, 66; strategies for, 68; themes,
     67

just-in-time training, 80

keys to team success: external client
     support, 63; internal district sup-
     port, 73; overview, 63; team mem-
     ber support, 63
key strategies: for external client sup-
     port partnerships, 87–89; for
     internal district support partner-
     ships, 77–79; for team member
     support partnerships, 65–77

leaders: concerns of team members,
     46; educational, v, vii, 14–15, 17;
     empowered, 27–29; major prob-
     lems of, 25–26; needs of, 77–78;
     real challenges of, 46; role of,
     19–20; ultimate challenge of, 3
leadership: new educational, vi, vii,
     13–16; quality, 92–93; shared,
     5–6, 19–20; team, 14–16; trans-
     formational, 96

motivation, intrinsic, 18–20

new team, ten steps to getting started,
     49–50

obstacles to teams, 25
open doors to successful teams, 63
openness: to new ideas, 78; to opin-
     ions, 78–79; See also respect and
     trust
organizational structures. See struc-
     tures, organizational
organizational systems. See systems,
     organizational
overview of keys: to team success,
     63; to team process, 45–46

paradigm shift, 92–93
Pareto chart, 71–72, 90, 95
partnerships: balanced, 91–92; exter-
     nal client support, 63, 86–89; sup-
     port of, 14; team member support
     of, 63, 65–67; team sponsor of,
     80–81; union leaders, 80
Plan-Do-Study-Act Cycle, 9, 71–73,
     74, 96
plus/delta strategy, 16, 17
power: balance of, 28, 91–93; team
     shared, 27–29, 92–93
project, completion of, 16, 50

Quality Empowerment Survey for
     Teams (QUEST): analysis of,
     52–59; QUEST solution (a diag-
     nostic prescriptive tool), 52
quality in education, 6–7, 13, 28–29,
     96

reality check, 92–93
recognition, 37, 38, 39, 40, 44–45,
     50, 83–84; questions to ask, 83;
     strategies for, 84; themes, 83
representation of essential groups,
     42, 85
resources and time: questions to ask,
     83; strategies for, 82–83; themes,
     82

resources for types of team training, 80

respect and trust, 43, 77–79; questions to ask, 77–78; strategies for, 79; themes, 78–79

rewards: project completion, 50; shifting attention of team, 17

run chart, 70, 73, 96

Scholtes, Peter S., 7, 26

Senge, Peter, 43

shared decision making, 18–20; questions to ask, 76; strategies for, 77; themes, 76–77

staff empowerment. *See* empowerment, staff

steps: to getting a new team started, 49–50; to team success, 41–45

strategies: external support partnerships, 86–87; internal district support partnerships, 79–86; simple and easy that work, 49–59; team member support partnerships, 65–79

structures, organizational, 85–86; questions to ask, 85; themes, 85–86

success. *See* teams, success in

systems, organizational, 84–85; improvement of, 90

teams: acceptance of, 37; advantages and benefits of, 5–7, 21–24; behavior of, 26; building, 27, 48–60, 84–85, 96; challenges, 77; challenges in education, v–vii; as change agents, 28; close of meetings, 16–17; considerations for improvement, 37, 38, 39, 40; and cooperative learning, 7–8; cross-functional, 7, 22–24, 26, 33; current efforts of, 33–46; data on, 34–36; disadvantages of, 24–26; empowerment model for education, 61–65, 65–91; environmental considerations for, 18–20; facilitator and facilitating, 50–52, 75–76; issues, 24–27; leader, 75–76; leadership, 14–16; overview of, 45–56; power of, 27–29, 93; problems with, 24–26; productive meetings, 50; questions to ask, 80; recognition of, 37, 38, 39, 40, 44–45, 50, 83–84; recurrent themes in, 36; resistance to, 24–26; rewards for, 5–6; seven steps to, 41–45; staff empowerment, 13–14; starting a new, 49–50; strategies for, 81; strengths of, 35–36; study result in, 40; success in, 7, 16; themes, 80–81; time for, 81–82; training, 16–18, 84–85

teaming: business of, 28–29; environmental considerations of, 13–20

teamwork, 4–7; follow-through on recommendations, 42–43; strategies for, 69; themes, 68

time, 41–42

tools of quality, 96

training. *See* teams, training

ultimate power of teams, 93

union leader partnerships, 25, 80

vision, v, 91–93

vision building, 18–20

About the Author

Mary Ann Smialek, Ed.D., is lead educational consultant for Quest Solutions in Pittsburgh, Pennsylvania. Her experience as an educator includes teaching at the elementary, middle school, and high school levels, and her published works include a variety of team-related subjects. Currently, Mary Ann is the editor of the American Society for Quality, Education Division QED NEWS. She facilitates successful team outcomes for education, business, and healthcare organizations. She can be reached at smialek@mail.com.